Compiled at Gordon Castle, Scotland,
and in Edinburgh and London
during the years 1828–1837

by

Georgiana McCrae

EDITED BY HUNTLY HIGGINS
AND BARBARA HIGGINS
*With prefaces by Brenda Niall
and Janet Hay*

SPECTRUM PUBLICATIONS

First Published 1996
by Spectrum Publications P/L
PO Box 75 Richmond Victoria Australia 3121
in conjunction with Huntly Higgins

Typeset by Spectrum Publications Pty Ltd

Cover: Montage incorporating miniature self-portrait by Georgiana McCrae and
her sketch of Gordon Castle, 1829; design by Sharyn Madder and Peter Shaw.

Cataloguing-in-Pulication data:

McCrae, Georgiana, 1804-1890
A commonplace book: compiled at Gordon Castle Scotland and
in Edinburgh and London during the years 1828-1837.

Includes index.
ISBN 0 86786 189 4

1. McCrae, Georgiana, 1804-1890 - Notebooks, sketchbooks,
etc. 2. Commonplace-books. 3. English poetry. 4. Women
painters - Victoria. I. Higgins, Huntly, 1917-
II. Higgins, Barbara, 1947-. III. Title.

994.5103092

Dedicated by the editors to the memory of Octavia
Frances Gordon Moore and Cora Frances Lucia Higgins,
through whom we learnt the story of Georgiana, the
Gordons and the McCraes.

Contents

Acknowledgements

The Editors are indebted to Georgiana's biographer, Dr Brenda Niall, for reading the manuscript and providing valuable information on a number of points regarding the life of the McCrae family and their relatives. She has also given us copies of enlightening documents such as the 5th Duke of Gordon's Disposition of the estate of Newton Garioch and Andrew McCrae's poem to his wife. Janet Hay has offered constant encouragement, for which we are most grateful. Judith Wright kindly lent us relevant manuscripts written by Georgiana. We also thank Barbara Blomfield, who copied Georgiana's sketch of her daughter Elizabeth for us, and Elizabeth Campbell, who made her collection of Georgiana relics available to us for inspection.

To both Brenda Niall and Janet Hay we give our sincere thanks for their sensitively written prefaces, in each case based on a profound knowledge of the author of this commonplace book.

The La Trobe Library, State Library of Victoria, The National Galleries of Scotland and Dr Denzil Ridgway kindly gave us permission to reproduce paintings or sketches in their possession, and we thank Ken Hosking for allowing us to use the computer-generated family trees.

The Editors are also grateful to those involved in the publication process, including Maria Rohr (Manager, Spectrum Publications) and her staff, Scott Howard (typesetting) and Peter Shaw (book design). Sharyn Madder was responsible for the original cover design. Peter and Matthew Higgins and Dr Gwyn Dow contributed useful comments on the draft of the Introduction. Linguistic help was received from Elizabeth Mayne (French) and Con Coroneos (Latin).

Prefaces

As we know from the novels of Fanny Burney and Jane Austen, young ladies of the late eighteenth and early nineteenth century were in the habit of collecting 'elegant extracts' from their reading and inscribing them in notebooks or 'commonplace books'. The collections might range from riddles and charades to more reflective matter such as extracts from sermons or philosophical treatises. Less consciously planned than an anthology, the commonplace book could nonetheless give a vivid sense of its owner's temperament and beliefs, her literary tastes and intellectual range. Georgiana Huntly Gordon (later Georgiana McCrae) left such a volume, which survives after more than one hundred and sixty years to show the breadth of her reading and the liveliness of her mind. Her great-grandson Dr Huntly Gordon Higgins and his daughter Barbara have given new life to Georgiana's notebook of 1828-37; with careful transcribing and unobtrusive editorial work they have produced what is in effect a map of Georgiana's mind. The Introduction provides the biographical background needed to understand why certain poems resonated for Georgiana so strongly that she wished to make them her own. Her grief at the death of her first child Elizabeth, in 1834, finds expression in her choice from poems by Burns, Mrs Hemans and others; and we may conjecture that she tried to console herself, as Shelley did in his own loss of a son, with the idea that love and loss are inextricably linked. Not all the poems in Georgiana's book yield easily to biographical interpretation, but all of them give insight into the mind and heart of this remarkably gifted woman. Her choices range from the intellectually demanding to the light-hearted: prose extracts from Goethe, a meditation on prayer, poems by Wordsworth and Shelley are interspersed with lines from anonymous and less able poets, epigrams and comic anecdotes of Scottish life. Her sense of history, her strong attachment to Scotland and her fluency in French are all apparent in this collection. As yet there is nothing of Australia. This book, which she brought with her when she sailed for Port Phillip in October 1840 on the ship **Argyle**, was one of her links with the past, stubbornly cherished in the years of what she described as her 'exile'. One of the entries commemorates the 'floure of souvenance', the forget-me-not. On the voyage to Australia a fellow-passenger on the **Argyle**, wishing to pay a graceful compliment to the ladies on board by likening each one to the flower she most resembled, spoke of Georgiana McCrae as the 'Scottish forget-me-not', This, then, is Georgiana's 'book of souvenance'.

—BRENDA NIALL

Georgiana McCrae has lived in the hearts and minds of her descendants for four and five generations. Her drawings, her paintings, her diaries — her stories and memories of her — have been treasured and passed from her children to their children down the generations.

For nearly half a century after her death in 1890 Georgiana was a strong family memory, fresh in the minds of her children and grandchildren but little known outside the McCrae family, their friends and some historians.

The intense childhood memory of his grandmother Georgiana and her dying wish *to be remembered* inspired her grandson (my grandfather) Hugh McCrae to publish 'Georgiana's Journal' in 1934. Now in its fourth edition, this volume provided a reference point for the family and brought Georgiana's life to the notice of the general public.

Thirty years later a strong sense of family prompted George McCrae to rescue his great-grandparents' homestead on the Mornington Peninsula, then disguised by the trappings of 1950's suburbia. Built to Georgiana's design this small slab building, vividly described in her diaries, is a visible frame for the life which Georgiana's resilient character made on this remote cattle run 'beyond the bounds of known civilisation'.

George McCrae worked to uncover the original building, collected McCrae memorabilia and welcomed the public. Through the generosity of George's son Andrew McCrae the Homestead became the property of the National Trust, to be preserved for the nation. It was extensively and exactly restored by the Trust and opened to the public on a regular basis in 1970.

Since then the collection of material relating to the McCraes has grown and will grow further with the recently opened Visitor Centre and Museum Room where paintings, drawings and fabrics can be displayed under controlled conditions.

The McCrae Homestead attracts many thousands of visitors each year and is cared for by a volunteer Committee of the National Trust dedicated to its preservation and to the memory of Georgiana. As these volunteer guides will tell you, it is astonishing how many people express an empathy with Georgiana — as wife, mother, pioneer, painter, observer — and admiration for her ability to find joy amongst the difficulties of pioneering life.

The La Trobe Library, State Library of Victoria, holds an extensive collection of McCrae family papers, relating particularly to three generations of literary and artistic talent: Georgiana, her son George Gordon McCrae and his son Hugh Raymond McCrae. These papers, together with those held by the National Trust, provide an enthralling family archive.

In 1994 Dr. Brenda Niall published her splendid book 'Georgiana: a biography of Georgiana McCrae, painter, diarist, pioneer'. The result of four years of intensive, skilful, professional research in Australia, England, Scotland and Switzerland distilled into a life of our remarkable ancestor this book, reading with the momentum of a good novel, nevertheless holds a comprehensive account of all that is yet known of Georgiana's life.

Georgiana's Commonplace Book, carefully treasured by the descendants of her daughter Frances, provides another dimension, a further insight into Georgiana's character: the thoughts, the influences which shaped her remarkable being. We are indebted to Georgiana's great-grandson, Huntly Higgins and her great-great-granddaughter Barbara for their skilful and patient transcription and for their wide-ranging research which brings Georgiana's Commonplace Book alive.

—*JANET HUNTLY HAY*
Founder, Georgiana McCrae Society

List of Illustrations

Georgiana, self-portrait
State Library of Victoria

Jane Graham, Georgiana's mother,
by Henry Hawkins, 1826
Dr Denzil Ridgway

Introduction: Georgiana's Life, Antecedents and Descendants

The source of this book is an old notebook, begun in 1828, and passed down from the author's daughter and granddaughter to her great grandson. For years the book lay unread with other family documents, until closer inspection revealed that it might hold something of interest and value for the present generation. So we set about the task of transcribing it and preparing it for publication.

Georgiana Huntly Gordon, artist, diarist and colonist, was born in London on 15th March 1804 in circumstances that, if not unusual, would then have been regarded as irregular. Her parents were Jane Graham, daughter of Ralph Graham of Rockmoor, and George Gordon, 8th Marquis of Huntly, later 5th Duke of Gordon. Jane maintained on her deathbed that she had been married to the Marquis and a family legend had it that the church in which this ceremony was said to have been performed had been subsequently burnt down with all its records. The far more likely situation is that the liaison was a natural one, unencumbered by formalities. However, in the Gordon tradition, Georgiana was acknowledged as the daughter of the Marquis, and during her childhood, adolescence and young womanhood received all the advantages of upbringing and education that were normally accorded a young lady of noble descent.

Georgiana's main accomplishments were in the artistic sphere, in painting and drawing, but she is also well known for her journal (1), which gives an unrivalled picture of early Melbourne society. The other main source of information about Georgiana and her times is the recent widely-acclaimed biography by Brenda Niall (2).

Georgiana spent much of her childhood in London, and glimpses of her early life are given in a series of articles by her grandson (3), 'Georgiana in England 1804–1829', described as having been 'built up and imagined by Hugh McCrae on a strong foundation of truth drawn from the diary of Georgiana Huntly Gordon'. She was educated first at a convent school kept by refugees from the French revolution, presided over by Madame la Comtesse d'Escouailles. Later, 'when suspicion arose that she was being converted to Roman Catholicism', she was removed to Claybrook House, Fulham and then to the New Road Boarding School (4), which was under the charge of a French Canadian lady. Georgiana became fluent in French and studied other languages, including Hebrew and Latin.

The articles on Georgiana in England purported to be a mixture of fact and imagination, so their biographical value is compromised by Hugh McCrae's literary licence. Take, for example, this description of part of a dream which Georgiana is supposed to have had about her Aunt Agnes, her mother's sister: 'At this point, my dream growing chaotic, Aunt Agnes' kisses became inextricably mixed up with roast beef and gooseberry pie, so that I was driven into taking a short cut through the Battle of Saratoga to the orchard outside. Then, on my way back, when I encountered M. Mauléon feeding the 1811 comet on Miss de Courcy's tartines and macaroons, I woke up.' Although M. Mauléon and Miss de Courcy were real people and the other elements of the dream were also part of Georgiana's experience, the account smacks very much of Hugh, who was much occupied with dreams. It may be added that the family records of the Gordons and the Grahams make no reference to an aunt called Agnes.

Georgiana was only eleven years old when she began taking lessons in painting from John Varley, the landscape painter, who was, by all accounts, a brilliant teacher(2). Varley was also an ardent astrologer and author of A Treatise on Zodiacal Physiognomy (1828). He was beset by many misfortunes, but his outlook on life is illustrated by a remark to a fellow painter, John Linnell, recorded by E.V.Lucas (5). In the midst of writs and imprisonment for debt and domestic embroilments, Varley was able to declaim: 'But all these troubles are necessary for me. If it were not for my troubles I would burst with joy.'. Frances Moore (née McCrae) wrote in the margin of a copy of Lucas' essays given to her son-in-law: 'John Varley taught our mother to paint in water colours—I had one of his pictures but sold it to my sister.'

Frances is known to have been in straitened circumstances after the death of her husband, George Moore.

Under Varley's tutelage Georgiana became highly accomplished in the pictorial arts, and was later a pupil of Dominic Serres, John Glover and Charles Hayter. She studied at the Royal Academy, and visited Gordon Castle each summer. A miniature portrait of her grandfather, the 4th Duke of Gordon, won her a silver medal from the Society for Promotion of Arts in 1821 when she was only seventeen. The following year she won a silver palette award for the most promising young portrait painter in Britain (4). She achieved recognition as a talented artist, and was quite prolific. In the years 1828-29 she painted some 50 portraits, 15 at Gordon Castle and 35 in Edinburgh. On her marriage she wrote in her diary 'Left my easel and changed my name.' Much later, in Melbourne in 1845, she wrote 'There is a living to be had here through my art of miniature painting, for which I have already several orders in hand, but dare not oppose the family wishes that money must not be made in that way!'.

Georgiana had considerable musical ability as a singer and pianist. Her daughter Frances recalled (6) in her later years that her mother sang such songs as 'There was a King in Thule', 'The Deep, Deep Sea', 'Auld Robin Gray' and 'The Land of the Leal' with admirable taste and feeling, assisted by the children's tutor with his flute, and, at times, by a visitor with a violin. French, Italian, Spanish and German ballads were all included in the repertoire, but her children were particularly stirred by the old Jacobite songs which their mother sang with such verve that 'a vision seemed to arise before them of the outlawed prince, his pale and haggard features pinched with hunger, a hunted look in the bonny blue eyes, as he crouched low in the heather and bracken, hiding in rocky caves known only to his faithful followers.' Even in her seventies, Georgiana could still captivate an audience with the feeling and expression of her songs.

Frances (Octavia Frances Gordon Moore, née McCrae) wrote in the family bible: 'Our mother lived from the age of 17 till 23 at Gordon Castle with the old Duke of Gordon. When the young Duke and Duchess came home she left one year after and ... was married to our father at Gordon

Castle....' The old Duke, when Georgiana was marriage, to Andrew writer to the signet place in 1830.

Georgiana's other children, named Ann elder of these, Gordon, who Admiral, Elizabeth they had three whom died un- without issue (7). of Ann Thomson, was born at Gordon Henri Sordet of sons. Thus Susan's lines represent of the last Duke of

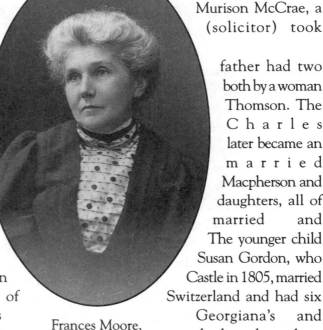

Frances Moore,
Georgiana's daughter

the 4th, died in 1827, 23, and Georgiana's Murison McCrae, a (solicitor) took

father had two both by a woman Thomson. The C h a r l e s later became an m a r r i e d Macpherson and daughters, all of married and The younger child Susan Gordon, who Castle in 1805, married Switzerland and had six Georgiana's and the direct descendants Gordon.

The 8th Marquis of Huntly, later the 5th Duke of Gordon, was a somewhat romantic figure, the first Colonel of the Gordon Highlanders and known throughout Scotland as the Cock o' the North. He was the 'Highland laddie' referred to in the song 'The Blue Bells of Scotland' (8):

> Oh, where, tell me where is your Highland
> laddie gone?
> He's gone with streaming banners where noble
> deeds are done,
> And my sad heart will tremble till he comes
> safely home.
> Ah, where, tell me where, did your Highland
> laddie stay?

The gate to Gordon Castle

George Gordon, 8th Marquis of
Huntly, later 5th Duke of Gordon,
Georgiana's father

He dwelt beneath the holly trees, beside the
　　rapid Spey,
And mony a blessing followed him the day he
　　went away.

He had in fact gone to Holland with his regiment; the holly trees were those in the gardens of Gordon Castle, which in Georgiana's time was a princely edifice, having been extensively rebuilt in the 18th century. Completed in 1776, the new buildings had a frontage of 568 feet, set in a vast park which had at one time been the Bog o' Gicht. In times past this had offered protection to the 'Gudeman o' the Bog', who 'secure in his tall tower in the middle of the Bog, protected by its causeway and its drawbridge' was the centre of authority 'benorth the Tay'(7).

We know little of Huntly's relationship with Jane Graham, which must remain for now a matter of speculation, although clues must exist somewhere in the archives of Scotland. Georgiana's daughter Frances,

Gordon Castle, 1830, by Georgiana McCrae
State Library of Victoria

6

whose personal integrity was beyond question, also wrote in the bible given to her by her mother: 'As there is no proof of the Duke's having married our grandmother, she (Georgiana) was always looked upon as a natural daughter, but her mother on her deathbed told our father that she was married to the Duke. There is no proof however and his relatives acknowledged no such marriage but circumstantial evidence would lead one to believe that such a marriage had taken place. Vide Family Record.' And again: 'Jane Graham, our maternal grandmother had met with an accident (fractured skull) falling out of a pony chase which affected her at times and so the marriage was probably set aside quietly.' The nature of the 'circumstantial evidence' is not known, although there are some grounds for speculation in relation to the extraordinary role played by the Duchess of Gordon (Elizabeth Brodie) in relation to the disposition of her husband's estate. This has been discussed by Niall (2), and will be mentioned later. The Family Record mentioned appears to be lost. Georgiana's grandmother, Jane Maxwell, refers enigmatically in a letter written in 1805 to 'the sham marriage performed and the divorce' (7). Dr. Niall (personal communication) thinks (though this is only inference drawn from a variety of sources as well as the context of the sentence) that she is referring to a 'one day marriage' of a certain Jean Christie, allegedly not consummated and later legally declared null and void. Jean was the mistress of Alexander, the 4th Duke. Many years later, and a few years after the death of Jane Maxwell, the Duke's first wife, Jean became the new Duchess.

We may also speculate that Jane Graham, Georgiana's mother, may have been 'affected' when she made her deathbed claim. The question of whether or not the marriage took place is of historical relevance mainly in connection with matters of inheritance. The most compelling evidence that it did not is that Georgiana herself never claimed legitimacy. This raises the question as to the identity of those who continued to promulgate the marriage story, which was apparently believed sincerely by at least one of Georgiana's children. One suspects that the McCrae family may have had a hand in this, as Andrew's sisters were known to embrace conventional Victorian values. However it is still something of a mystery why Georgiana herself, who lived to be 86, did not apprise her children of the true situation. At all events the union between George and Jane, whatever its nature—marriage, 'as he met her once a Maying' or something in between—led to a most successful outcome in the person of Georgiana Gordon. One is reminded of the lines of Laurence Hope (9):

> Who scans his pedigree, nor shrinks to trace
>> Some link unlawful? Yet he had not been
> Had this illicit love not taken place,
>> Or that forbidden face remained unseen.

With the death of the 5th Duke of Gordon in 1836 the title lapsed, the Duchess, the former Elizabeth Brodie, having had no children. Much later, in 1875, Queen Victoria revived the title by conferring it on the 6th Duke of Richmond, Charles Lennox, a grandson of Charlotte Gordon, Georgiana's aunt, who married the 4th Duke of Richmond. Charlotte is known to history as the hostess at the famous ball held in Brussels on the eve of the Battle of Waterloo, described by Byron in Childe Harold Canto III:

> There was a sound of revelry by night
> And Belgium's capital had gathered there
> Her beauty and her chivalry...

Incidentally it may be of interest to monarchists to learn that both Charlotte and her sister Georgina, who married John Russell, 6th Duke of Bedford, are great-great-great-great-grandmothers of the Princess of Wales, through her paternal grandmother, and hence (5 greats) grandmothers of one of the heirs apparent to the throne.

Georgiana's eldest son, George Gordon McCrae, travelled to Scotland after the death of the Duchess of Gordon (Elizabeth) in 1864, ostensibly to press the family's claims, but apparently it was not a vigorous advocacy, perhaps because his case was weak. It was also said that he was received so warmly and entertained so lavishly that he either forgot the purpose of his mission or considered it inappropriate to pursue the matter. Furthermore he was primarily concerned with his literary work and wrote extensively on his travels; he also collected material for other books, such as 'The Man in the Iron Mask'.

A Literary Tradition

This brings us to the literary tradition which Georgiana both inherited and passed on to her descendants. It would be nice to think that James I of Scotland (1396–1437) had some slight influence, as his daughter became a progenitor of the Gordon line by marrying the 2nd Earl of Huntly, the Lord High Chancellor of Scotland. However the genes would have been diluted, as it were, by a factor of 8192 by the time they reached Georgiana, James' (11 greats) granddaughter. According to the Dictionary of English History (10) James was the only poet of real genius in either England or Scotland during the fifteenth century. Be this as it may, he was a great poet as well as a great king, 'a man altogether in advance of his age—a lover of civilization, order and law, as well as of scholarship and poetry' (11). Some historians, however, have seen him as something of a tyrant in view of the stern treatment, including execution and forfeiture of estates, which he meted out to various nobles, including some Highland chiefs. James' autobiographical poem, The Kings Quare, or Kingis Quhair, written while he was a prisoner of the English in Windsor Castle, describes his delight at first glimpsing his future wife, Lady Jane Beaufort (John of Gaunt's granddaughter), through his prison bars:

> And therewith cast I down my eye again
> Where as I saw walking under the tower
> Full secretly, now comen here to pleyne
> The fairest or the freshest youngé flower
> That e'er I saw, methought, before that hour;
> To sene her part, and follow I na might
> Methought the day was turnéd into night.

Byron was also related to the leaders of the Gordon clan through his mother, who was descended, through the Gordons of Gicht, from the 2nd Earl of Huntly. Thus two of the great poets in the English language,

Byron and James I of Scotland, are related in a direct line. And Georgiana's grandfather, the 4th Duke of Gordon, was a passable poet in the Scottish idiom, much in the tradition of Burns, his friend and protégé. He has been described, perhaps with some ambiguity, as occupying 'an honourable place in the front rank of Scotia's minor poets' (7). These lines are from a rather pretentious elegy by his daughter Jessie:

> In poetry he showed great taste and skill
> Whene'er he chose to climb Parnassus' Hill.

Georgiana herself is of course best known in the literary sense for her diary 'Georgiana's Journal' (1), which was edited by her grandson, Hugh McCrae, and published in 1934. The Journal is an important document in respect to the early history of Melbourne and of the nearby Mornington Peninsula where Andrew McCrae settled in 1844 at the spot which now bears his name. In his Introduction to the first edition W.B.Dalley compared Georgiana with Isobella Beeton and George du Maurier as among the shrewdest annalists of what he called 'The Victorian Household'. 'The affinity between the three is singular', he wrote. 'They were artists to their finger-tips. Each knew that art is the elimination of superfluities; each had the eye of a lynx for the significant.'

It is hoped that the present volume may form some sort of an adjunct to Niall's biography and to the Journal, which does not commence until just before Georgiana's departure for Australia in 1840, if only for the portrayal of Georgiana's attitudes as a young woman. Of course 'Georgiana in England' represents a still earlier period, but it was written in later life. Brenda Niall writes 'In 1828 Georgiana had been a romantic; in 1841 she is an ironist' (2). This commonplace book contains ample evidence of a romantic outlook, and to a lesser extent, of a growing sense of irony.

Georgiana's direct influence on Australian life was considerable, but a fuller appreciation of the impact which she and her husband made on the young colony, and particularly its cultural development, may be obtained from what we know of the lives of their children and other descendants.

George Gordon McCrae, Georgiana's eldest son

George Gordon McCrae was the eldest surviving child of Georgiana and Andrew. The first-born, a daughter, had died in infancy. George became known as the 'Father of Victorian Poetry' (referring of course to the Australian State rather than the Victorian era). He 'was for half a century the outstanding literary figure in Melbourne' (12), although some of his friends and contemporaries, such as Adam Lindsay Gordon, Marcus Clarke and Henry Kendall are much better known to posterity. It is said (13) that he dominated by dint of a gracious personality, who gave and enjoyed friendship. His literary accomplishments are well documented, e.g. (12, 14). Of particular note, perhaps, is that two of his long poems, Mamba and The Story of Balladeadro are 'the first Australian poems of any importance whose themes are aboriginal' (12). As a boy at Arthur's seat, on the Mornington Peninsula in Victoria, McCrae had befriended and played with Aborigines, with whom he and his family had great sympathy. Kendall described the Aboriginal poems as ones which only McCrae could write, but they have been criticised by Green (12) as being too much in the manner of Scott's narrative poems and not depicting the Aborigine as he really is. It is not unnatural that the Scottish-born McCrae, who had been tutored by another Scot, Mr McLure, as well as by his parents, would have introduced some Scottish romanticism into his work, but it is difficult to accept that his distinguished critic, although himself a poet and scholar and librarian at Sydney University, would have had a better knowledge than McCrae of what the Aborigines were really like before the colonial onslaught began in Victoria. Healy (15) has given us a detailed and balanced assessment of McCrae's excursions into Aboriginal culture, concluding that he had a sufficient sense of myth as an expressive medium, which must be the point of entry into the Aboriginal mind for white Australia. Consequently his reaching out for it was more authentic than his own or subsequent generations have recognized.

G.G.McCrae was also quite accomplished at painting and drawing; he was elected honorary secretary of the Victorian Society of Fine Arts in 1856, and exhibited at its exhibition in 1857 (16). He was an illustrator of books (14), and Sir Oswald Brierley, a visitor in 1842 to the home of Andrew and Georgiana McCrae in Melbourne, and later to become marine painter to Queen Victoria and Curator of the Painted Hall, Greenwich, said that if George had devoted himself entirely to the representation of ships he would have made his mark as a maritime painter (17). A painting of Ben Boyd's schooner 'Wanderer', which has come down to us, is to be attributed either to George or to Brierley himself, who was associated with Boyd as manager of his factory at Eden. The painting itself does not closely resemble Brierley's lithograph of the 'Wanderer', as reproduced in Georgiana's Journal (1).

George's son Hugh outshone his father to become one of Australia's most notable poets. He was also a talented illustrator, and artistic ability was passed on to his daughters Mahdi and Rose ('Smee'). A good review of the life and work of Hugh McCrae is given by Green (12) concluding with the words: 'It is difficult to imagine that any poet working within his limits will ever surpass him in his own kind'. And: 'It is possible that his work may, like Herrick's, outlast that of poets who are not so limited through sheer perfection in its kind' (13). Phillips (18) has given us some idea of the perceived limitations, but despite these McCrae is an English-language poet of the first rank. 'The Outline of Literature' (Ed. John Drinkwater, revised edition 1966) refers to his poetry as 'sensuous and passionate with a great sense of verbal magic'. Green writes: 'As lyrists McCrae and Neilson were unapproachable in Australia until the appearance of Judith Wright... And compared to Neilson it is McCrae who is the finer craftsman, finer by far.' For another appreciation of McCrae's life and work see the tributes to him in Meanjin (19) by Robert Fitzgerald, Nettie Palmer, Jack Lindsay and T.Inglis Moore. And Norman Lindsay wrote (20) that 'the poetry of Hugh McCrae has one especial claim on our gratitude and reverence. It is the first poetry written in this country which has the quality we call major'. But Hugh was not universally admired: Dutton (21) refers to the 'bogus vitalism' of McCrae and Lindsay, but includes two of Hugh's poems in his anthology, while acknowledging that Slessor thought very highly of McCrae and that Judith Wright had written of him with admiration. Nettie Palmer also recorded (22) that A.G. Stephens 'admired McCrae consistently' but put Neilson first among the lyricists. It is sometimes forgotten that Hugh was also a master of prose (23), although he did not publish extensively in this medium. He is the only Australian included in 'The Oxford Book of Letters'.

Hugh's sister, Dorothy Frances McCrae, shared the literary heritage, and published several volumes of lyrics, which according to Miller (14) claim attention 'if only for the revelation of a gracious, translucent personality'. An examination of some of her best poems suggests that she may have been somewhat underrated; her efforts could well have escaped attention as she lived and worked in the shadow of a notable father and a flamboyant yet illustrious brother. George's sister, Frances Moore, and Frances' daughter, Cora Higgins (1885-1979) both published short stories and wrote verse, but neither had any serious literary pretensions. Frances' son, James Lorenzo Moore, did not follow exactly in the literary tradition of the Gordons and McCraes, but he published an interesting book, 'The Canine King', on the breeding and training of sheepdogs, a subject on which he was an authority. Gilbert Mant, a grandson of Georgiana's son Farquhar Peregrine (Perry) was born in 1902, and has been a journalist for many years; by 1992 he had written twelve books, four of which were published in that year. On the death of Harold Larwood in 1995, Mant, aged 93, was able to pay a tribute as the only surviving journalist of the body-line series.

Georgiana clearly influenced the development of George Gordon McCrae's literary talents, and through him Hugh's notable achievements. She was not a poet of any consequence herself, but her appreciation and love of poetry is clearly revealed in the present volume. Although her main talents lay in other directions she was a vital link in the transmission of the literary tradition.

Similarly, Georgiana may be said to have founded an artistic tradition which was followed by many of her descendants.

The Gordon Heritage

As Brenda Niall has shown (2) the Gordon Heritage contributed greatly to Georgiana's evaluation of her own identity. Her full acceptance by her father and grandfather strengthened her ties with the past, and her later rejection by the interloper Elizabeth Brodie, her father's widow, induced considerable bitterness on two counts: the challenge to her place in the Gordon family hierarchy and the almost illegal and certainly immoral way in which she had been deprived of her just inheritance against the expressed wishes of her late father.

Georgiana's direct ancestors on the Gordon side include many people prominent in Scottish history, such as Robert the Bruce, William Wallace and Walter the Steward, the ancestor of the Stewart kings. Her pride in the family heritage is shown in an unpublished manuscript in her handwriting, probably compiled from Gordon Castle records, in which the main characters and events in the Gordon saga are systematically recorded. In the rest of this section any reference in quotes is to be attributed to this manuscript, which, together with the published history references, is the main source of information.

The Gordon line is considered to have 'begun' in Britain with Adam de Gourdon. Although described in ancient records as a Norman, he came from a region well to the south of Normandy, being a cadet of de Gourdon of Castel de Gourdon near Chaluz, or Chalus, about 30 km from Limoges and about 110 km NNW of the town of Gourdon. Well before the Battle of Hastings, Adam is supposed to have accompanied Malcolm Canmore when Macbeth was slain in 1057 and Canmore crowned Malcolm III in 1058. He obtained a grant of lands in Berwickshire, near Coldstream, where he settled; these lands were still

14

known as East and West Gourdoun in the 19th century. Adam was killed at the siege of Alnwick in 1093.

Only sketchy accounts remain of the next few generations. Another Adam de Gourdon gave certain lands to the Abbey of Kelso for the purpose of a cemetery. His son Richard (or Bertrand) died in 1200. His son Thomas de Gourdon died about 1230. His son, also Thomas, died in 1260 and was succeeded by his only child Alicia. She married her cousin, who joined the Earls of Carrick and Atholl in a crusade and died at Tunis in 1269. Their son Adam married Marjorie, daughter of Sir George Huntly of Frowcester, Co. Gloucester, thus introducing the Huntly name to the Gordon line. Adam died in 1295, 'as proved by a passport to Marjory (*sic*) wife of the late Adam Gordon—to go to England'.

Their son, Sir Adam Gordon, or de Gourdon, was Warden of the Marches in 1300 and Justiciar of Lothian under Edward I. He supported Robert the Bruce at Bannockburn in 1314, and was afterwards granted the lands in Aberdeenshire centred on Strathbogie (referred to by Georgiana by the alternative spelling of Strathbolgie), which later became known as Huntly. Adam was Bruce's Ambassador to the Pope in 1320, and was killed at the Battle of Halidon Hill in 1333. His eldest son Alexander was present at Halidon but escaped. He was killed at the Battle of Durham in 1346. Another Adam de Gourdon who appears in the family tree was known as Black Adam of Auchindoun. A study of family trees and historical dates suggests that he was possibly one of the four sons of Sir Adam Gordon. Another son, William, was ancestor of the family of Kenmure, and a daughter married Hamilton of Cadzow, ancestor of the Dukes of Hamilton.

Alexander's son John was taken prisoner with King David I at Durham, and not released until 1357, William, 1st Earl of Douglas being bound as one of his sureties. He was succeeded by his son John de Gourdon, who had some notable military successes against the English, defeating Sir John Lillburn and taking him prisoner in 1371, attacking Sir Thomas Musgrove and taking him prisoner in 1372, and taking Berwick by surprise 'with a handful of men' in 1378. In a new grant of the lands of Strathbolgie Co. Aberdeen by King Robert II in 1376 he is designated Joannes de Gordon, 'now being first altered from the Norman patronymic de Gourdon'. The Estate is granted 'to him and his heirs Whatsomever'. He was killed at the Battle of Otterburn in 1388. In Georgiana's account of these events, the word Whatsomever is capitalized and underlined.

So it was not until 1376 that the Gordons finally settled down in occupation of their northern estate (24). John was succeeded by his only legitimate son, Adam, the last in the male line of the Gordons of Huntly and Strathbogie, who married Elizabeth, daughter of Sir William Keith, Great Marischall (Marshal) of Scotland. At the Battle of Homildon Hill in 1402, Adam was slain in heroic circumstances, as described on page 88 by Pinkerton and by Scott in his dramatic piece 'Halidon Hill'. (Scott's reasons for using the name of an earlier battle, in 1333, are mentioned in the Notes).

Adam Gordon was succeeded by his daughter, Elizabeth, who was permitted by the phrase 'to ... heirs Whatsomever' in the Charter of 1376 to inherit the estates of Strathbolgie and the other estates of Gordon and Huntly in Berwickshire. In 1408 Elizabeth married Sir Alexander de Seton, a descendant of Christina, Bruce's sister, and her husband, Sir Christopher de Seton, who had assisted Bruce at the skirmish at Methven in 1306, and subsequently. (Georgiana was also a direct descendant of Robert the Bruce through the Stewarts). Alexander was a hostage for King James I of Scots in 1422. A daughter, Elizabeth, married the Earl of Ross. The eldest son, also Alexander de Seton, Lord Gordon and Huntly, was created 1st Earl of Huntlie in 1449 by James II of Scotland, 'with limitations to the heirs male by his third wife (Elizabeth, daughter of Lord Crichton) and they to take the name of Gordon'. His promotion was a reward for his services against the Douglas faction (10). He eventually defeated the Earl of Crauford, one of the Douglas allies, at the battle of Brechin in 1452, but his two younger brothers were killed in the conflict. One of these was ancestor of the Setons of Meldrum.

During the ensuing centuries the Earls and Marquises of Huntly and the Dukes of Gordon and their relatives (including lords of Sutherland, Lochinvar, Kenmure, Aboyne, and Aberdeen) espoused a variety of causes, sometimes for and sometimes against Catholicism, both in support of and in opposition to the English and Scottish monarchs, and in pursuit of clan rivalries.

Alexander de Seton died in 1470, and was succeeded by his eldest son, George (Seton) Gordon, 2nd Earl of Huntlie and Lord High Chancellor of Scotland. He married the widow of the Earl of Angus, a daughter of King James I of Scotland. They had six daughters and four sons. The eldest daughter, the beautiful Lady Catherine Gordon, known as the 'White Rose of Scotland', was bestowed in marriage by her cousin, James IV, upon the English pretender, Perkin Warbeck, whom James believed to be the Duke of York, the rightful heir to the English throne (10). The wedding took place in January 1496 with much pomp at Huntly Castle, Strathbogie, which had been but recently rebuilt. Catherine was later taken prisoner with her husband by Henry VII, and became an attendant to the Queen (8). After Warbeck's execution in 1499 she married in succession, James Strangeways, Sir Matthew Cradock (or Craddock), ancestor of the Earls of Pembroke, and Christopher Ashton.

This family, and other generations of Gordons, illustrate the closely interlocked nature of the Scottish aristocracy and gentry. Among George's sons-in-law were Lord Lyndsay, Lord Gray, and various knights or baronets, some of them progenitors of noble lines. George's second son married the Countess of Sutherland and became Earl of Sutherland, ancestor of the Dukes of Sutherland. Sir William Gordon, the third son, was ancestor of the Gordons of Gicht, from whom Byron was descended. Sir James Gordon, the fourth son, of Latterfourie, was the Premier Baronet of Scotland.

Strathbogie, on the Deveron River in Aberdeenshire, later became known as Huntly. It was the main seat of the Gordons until Gordon Castle, at Fochabers, on Moray Firth near the mouth of the River Spey, was completed in 1498 by the 2nd Earl, who died in 1507.

His eldest son, Alexander, the 3rd Earl of Huntly, married Janet, daughter of John Stuart, Earl of Atholl. They had three sons and four daughters. One son was ancestor of the Gordons of Cluny, another became Bishop of Aberdeen. The daughters married Colin, Earl of Argyll, Lord

Gray, Lord Invermeath and Menzies of Weem. The eldest son, John Gordon, married Jane, the illegitimate daughter of James IV, and they had two sons, one of whom became Bishop of Galloway. John never succeeded to the lands and titles, as he died in 1517, six years before his father.

John's elder son, George Gordon, succeeded his grandfather to become the 4th Earl of Huntly. He married Elizabeth Keith, descendant of William, Earl Marischall and had issue, seven sons and three daughters. He was a soldier of note, defeating the English troops in 1542 (10). However he suffered defeat at Pinkie in 1547, which he dubbed 'the rough wooing'—a term later applied to the whole campaign. He was a Privy Counsellor and one of the Lords of Regency in Scotland (1536), Lieutenant of the North, Captain General of the Forces (1537) and Lord High Chancellor of Scotland (1546-49 and 1561-62). His daughter Jane married Bothwell, who divorced her before his marriage to the Queen. Jane later married her cousin Alexander, Earl of Sutherland.

Following a dispute with Mary, who had deprived him of the earldom of Moray in 1562, Huntly denied her admittance to her castle of Inverness, which he then held, but shortly afterwards he was defeated at the battle of Corrichie, where he was leading the rebellious Highlanders. He died the same day, probably of a heart attack; he was extremely overweight. Mary's forces were under the command of the Earl of Moray. One of Huntly's sons, Sir John Gordon, was captured and convicted of treason, 'this through the jealousy of his brother-in-law The Infamous Bothwell', and beheaded at Aberdeen. It availed him nought that in earlier times he had been one of Mary's numerous suitors, described in Georgiana's manuscript as 'Queen Marie's luve', a phrase evidently taken from ancient records.

The family estates were forfeited to the crown after Corrichie, but in 1565 they were restored to George's eldest son, also George, 5th Earl of Huntly, who was Chancellor in 1564-67. He married Anne, daughter of James Hamilton, Duke of Chatelharault, 'and had issue by her one son and one daughter Jane, who married George, Earl of Caithness'. After the murder of Darnley, the father of James VI (James I of England), which he is said to have abetted, the 5th Earl accompanied Mary to Seton and was one of the councillors who presided at Bothwell's trial. He died in 1576 of a seizure during a game of football.

His son, also George, the 6th Earl, was a supporter of the King and was created 1st Marquis of Huntly in 1599. He married Henrietta, daughter of Esme Stuart, Duke of Lennox, and niece of King James V. He had a turbulent career; he was accused of being in league with Phillip of Spain, was a signatory to the Spanish blanks and, in continuation of the family feud, put the 'bonny Earl' of Moray to death in 1592. He defeated the Earl of Argyle but later effected a reconciliation with him. Charles I attempted to curb Huntly's influence by depriving him of his shrievalties of Aberdeen and Inverness. The 1st Marquis died in 1636, and was succeeded by his only son George.

The relationship between the Gordons and the Campbell clan was sometimes close, at others hostile. It is recorded (10) that 'the settlement of the Highlands was largely assisted by using the influence of two great families—the Huntlys and the Argyles—who, though Lowland in their origin, had by marriage or other means been gradually acquiring immense possessions and influence in the Highland districts; and this influence James (IV—Ed.) did not scruple to manipulate, so far as he could for the purpose of strengthening the royal authority in those remote parts'. The 2nd Marquis of Huntly married Anne, the daughter of Archibald, 7th Earl of Argyle, so that the earlier injection of Stewart genes into the Gordon line was now to be reinforced with those of the Campbells. Nevertheless, after being appointed Charles I's lieutenant and having rejected the overtures of the covenanters, Huntly took the field against Argyle. Later he refused to lay down his arms, even at the command of the King, who was under the control of Parliament. Eventually he was taken prisoner, and beheaded by the Covenanters at Edinburgh in 1649, seven weeks after Charles himself lost his head at Whitehall.

The children of the 2nd Marquis of Huntly again illustrate how the Gordon genes were being distributed throughout the Scottish nobility, and even more widely. There were five daughters and five sons. Of the daughters, Anne married James, Earl of Perth, Henrietta married first George, Lord Seton, and second John, Earl of Traquair, Jean married the Earl of Haddington, Mary married Irvine of Drum, and Catherine, the youngest, married Andrzej Morsztyn, Grand Treasurer of Poland in 1659. Their descendant Stanislaw August Poniatowski, the last King of Poland, is often remembered for his association with Catherine the Great of Russia. Of the sons, George, the eldest, was killed at the Battle of Alford in 1645; Lewis ('the 'Lewie Gordon' of the auld song') succeeded his father; Charles was created Earl of Aboyne in 1660 and was ancestor of later Marquises of Huntly; James 'retired' to France during the 'Usurpation'; Henry served as a cavalry officer in Poland.

The legitimate lines of descent were supplemented by a parallel distribution of Gordon genes throughout the population by extranuptial liaisons. Thus in an isolated country such as Scotland, in the days before travel became common and with no successful invasions for many hundreds of years, the national identity was immensely reinforced by the development of a network of biological relationships. These may have been stronger within the aristocracy but they nevertheless pervaded the whole of society. Everyone was literally related to everyone else, although many of these relationships were very poorly recorded and documented. Where appropriate records have been kept, even imperfectly, it is apparent that there are multiple relationships between any two individuals. In this sense the aristocracy has performed a useful service in providing data which can help us confirm the strength of the biological network, and incidentally help in disposing of the myth that any particular line of descent warrants a claim to preeminence.

Lewis, the 3rd Marquis of Huntly, married Isabel, daughter of Sir James Grant of Grant. They had a son, George, and three daughters: Ann, who married Count de Crolly; Mary, who married, first, Adam Urquhart of Meldrum, and second, James, Earl of Perth; and Jean, who married the 4th Earl of Dumfermline 'who was forfeited in 1690'. Lewis was restored by Charles II to the Honours in 1651, but did not obtain possession of any part of the estate. After his death in 1663 an annuity of 250 pounds was allowed for his widow.

George, the 4th Marquis of Huntly married Elizabeth Howard, daughter of Henry, Duke of Norfolk. Their daughter Jean married James, Earl of Perth. George was restored by the Parliament to the full family Honours and Estate in 1664, and he was created Duke of Gordon in 1684. He was Governor of Edinburgh Castle in 1688 and valiantly defended it on behalf of King James in 1689, after being summoned to surrender by the Scotch Convention. Macaulay (25) records how Gordon was solicited to fire on the city, but 'positively refused to take on himself so grave a responsibility on no better warrant than the request of a small cabal.'

'On one occasion' Macaulay writes 'his drums beat a parley: the white flag was hung out: a conference took place; and he gravely informed the enemy that all his cards had been thumbed to pieces, and begged to have a few more packs '. This request was granted. At length supplies were exhausted and after a siege of three months the Castle was 'surrendered upon honorable terms of capitulation'.

The Duke died in 1716 and was succeeded by his son Alexander, who married Henrietta Mordaunt, daughter of the Earl of Peterborough and Monmouth. They had issue four sons and seven daughters, of whom Georgiana lists the fate of only six. Three of the daughters died unmarried: Henrietta, Jean and Charlotte. Anne, Betty and Catharine married respectively William, Earl of Aberdeen, Mr. Shelly, Rector of Stocktown and Francis Charteris Esq. of Amisfield. The second son, Lord Charles, was an officer in the British Service and died unmarried in 1779, 'after being long insane'. The third son, Lord Adam of Preston Hall, was a Lt.General in the British Army, Colonel of the 1st Regiment of Foot and Governor of Clifford Fort, M.P. for the Counties of Aberdeen and Kincardine 'successively during several Parliaments'. He married Jean, Duchess Dowager of Atholl ('better known as 'Laik of Gold'- from the fact of her having jilted Dr. Austin for the Duke of Atholl—on which event the Dr. composed the Immortal Song'). Alexander's fourth son, Lord Lewis, died unmarried in 1747. The eldest son Cosmo George became the 3rd Duke of Gordon on the death of his father in 1728.

The 2nd Duke of Gordon had not enjoyed an illustrious military career, as many of his ancestors had done. Fighting at Sherriffmuir in

1715 on behalf of the Stewart cause he was even accused of cowardice in the ballad quoted by George Gordon (7):

> Wha' wad hae thocht the Gordon gay
> That day wad quit the green, man?
> Auchluncart and Auchanochie
> Wi' a' the Gordon tribe, man.

The situation at Sherriffmuir was actually quite complex. The Royalist army, mainly regulars, were under the command of The Duke of Argyle; the Jacobite forces, consisting mainly of Highlanders, were under the Earl of Mar. The left wing of the Royalist troops were defeated by the MacDonalds, who formed the centre of the Jacobite army, while Argyle himself and the dragoons defeated the left wing of their opponents, but then withdrew for fear of being cut off. The day went to the Highlanders, but their victory was not decisive, and there was much confusion (10).

Henrietta Mordaunt is one of the more notable women in Georgiana's lineage. She is credited with introducing many agricultural improvements to Banffshire, including the fallowing and making of hay. In 1735 she was given a pension of 1000 pounds per year by the Government, which ceased abruptly in 1745 as a consequence of the treasonable behaviour of her younger son, Lord Lewis Gordon, who had joined Prince Charles, and her showing favour to the Young Pretender by setting out a breakfast for him as he passed the park gates of Preston Hall, her home near Edinburgh, on his march to England at the end of October, 1745 (7). Her portrait, by Kneller, was part of the Gordon Castle collection, and Georgiana and her grandfather, the 4th Duke, were to agree that among the hundreds of Gordon family portraits it was the one which most resembled Georgiana herself in face and figure (2). Henrietta's portrait bust in bas-relief is to be found on the south wall of Elgin Cathedral, near the burial vault of the Gordons. (Over the vault is the monument to the 1st Earl of Huntly with a Latin inscription recording that he died at Huntly (*apud huntlie*) on 15th July 1470.)

Alexander was 'a pious Romanist, like all his ancestors'. His son, Cosmo was brought up 'in the doctrines of the Church of England' by his mother after his father's death, when he became the 3rd Duke of Gordon, and he supported the Hanoverian cause in 1745. At the same time his younger brother, Lewis, was active and influential on behalf of the Jacobite forces in the north of Scotland (7), fought at Culloden as a battalion commander, survived and eventually escaped to France, never to return to Scotland. The two other brothers, Charles and Adam, served the Hanoverian King George.

Cosmo married a relative, Lady Katharine Gordon of Haddo, daughter of the Earl of Aberdeen, and had issue three daughters and three sons. The daughters, Susan, Anne and Catharine married respectively Thomas, Earl of Westmoreland, the Revd. Chalmers, Minister of Cairney and Mr. Booker. William, the second son, Lord Vice Admiral of Scotland and M.P. for the shires of Moray and Inverness, married a daughter of Viscount Irvine. Lord George, the third son, of whom more later, was the leader of the notorious Gordon Riots. The eldest son, Alexander, became the 4th Duke of Gordon on Cosmo's death in France in 1752 at the age of 42. The new Duke was only nine years old, and he was to reign for seventy five years. In 1756 his mother the Duchess Katherine married an American, General Staats Long Morris—'a worthy man who with their uncle Lord Adam Gordon watched over the interests of his stepson so well that on his coming of age, 17th June 1764, he had 30 000 pounds cash lying at his bankers for immediate wants.'

Of Georgiana's more immediate ancestors on the Gordon side, the greatest interest attaches to her grandparents Alexander, the 4th Duke, and his first wife, Jane Maxwell, daughter of Sir William Maxwell of Monreith and his wife, a member of the Blair family of Blair. Jane had five daughters and two sons. The eldest daughter Charlotte, born in 1768, Countess of Enzie in her own right, married Charles Lennox, 4th Duke of Richmond; Madelina married first Sir John Sinclair, and second Charles Fysche Palmer Esq., M.P. for Luton, Bedfordshire; Susan married William, Duke of Manchester; Louisa married Charles, Marquis of Cornwallis; and Georgiana married John Russell, 6th Duke of Bedford. The younger son, Lord Alexander Gordon, died unmarried in 1807 at the age of 23. The elder son, George, 8th Marquis of Huntly, later became the 5th Duke of Gordon.

As a supporter of the Hanoverian kings the 4th Duke received various favours: for example George III appointed him Keeper of the Grand Seal of Scotland, for which onerous duty he received 3000 pounds a year. He was created a peer of Great Britain in 1784 by the titles of Earl of Norwich and Lord Gordon of Huntly in Gloucestershire. He was a Knight of the Thistle and Colonel of the Regiment of 'Northern Fencibles'.

The Duke was the father of 16 children, of whom seven were by his first Duchess, Jane, between 1768 and 1785, and five by Jean Christie, between 1791 and 1810. However he made no distinction between his children, in accordance with the Gordon custom, so that their upbringing led to no sense of superiority or inferiority on the basis of legitimacy. Jane Maxwell, also, treated the children equally, but referred to her son, the Duke's heir, as 'my George', and his elder half-brother, also George, as 'the Duke's George'(7).

Alexander appears to have been extremely popular and he clearly had many admirable qualities, some of which became evident during the iniquitous 'clearances' in northern Scotland during the period from about 1814 to 1821. The callousness with which the small tenants of the county of Sutherland were ejected, and their homes burnt, so that their land might be turned into more profitable sheep-runs has been described by McLeod (26). However the system of merging crofts and small farms into larger units did not take place on Gordon land (7). At a meeting with the Factors in 1821 the Duke was urged to do away with certain crofts, and add the land to neighbouring farms. On asking what would happen to the dispossessed he was told that they would just have to look for a living elsewhere. After an adjournment for lunch Alexander said he had considered the matter of how to dispose of the people: 'We will take them and drown them in Deveron. If we deprive them of the means of making their livelihood, it would be the most humane course', adding 'they or their forebears were there before me, and will be there after I am gone. They must not be cast adrift; they will retain their holdings.' And there the matter ended (7). The Duke's liberal outlook (although in politics he was a Tory) is also shown in letters to William Tod, his private secretary and Factor for one of the estates, in which he expresses pity for the tenants after a bad harvest and an inclination to relieve their want, and enjoins Tod to take care that no abuse is committed. His attitude to the clearances was also consistent with a desire to maintain feudal relationships (27), which may well have been a stronger motive than the prospects for immediate enrichment which the establishment of large sheep runs would have ensured.

Jane Maxwell was an outstanding woman, in appearance and personality, in her joie-de-vivre and in her emotional intensity. The Earl of Buchan addressed her in verses beginning:

Thou beauteous star whose silvery light
Enchanting came upon my youthful sight (7).

She has been described (7) as 'incomparable', 'dazzling', 'glamorous', a 'politico-society hostess par excellence' and as having 'acute political intuition, allied to a stunning beauty and ready wit'. She has been immortalized in paintings by Reynolds and Romney, but Jane's daughter Louisa considered that the best portrait of her mother was one by W. Smith, a copy of which was made by Georgiana (1). In his beautiful portrait of Jane and her son George, reproduced here in black and white, Romney achieved a perfect likeness, according to Georgiana. Another well-known picture shows Jane 'holding court' in Edinburgh, with Burns reciting his poems; in yet another she is in highland garb, on a white horse, recruiting for the Gordon Highlanders in 1794. The success of the campaign to raise a regiment is said to have been influenced by her inviting likely recruits to accept the King's Shilling from between her teeth by way of a kiss. Although denied by her daughter Madelina (7), the story is an integral part of the history of the Gordon Highlanders and is popularly accepted in Scotland.

Romney's portrait of Jane Maxwell, Duchess of Gordon, Georgiana's
grandmother, with her son George, Georgiana's father
National Galleries of Scotland

Jane had an eventful life, and knew much sorrow (7). As a girl of seventeen the 'Flower of Galloway' had fallen in love with a young army officer, who was sent abroad and later reported dead. A year or so later she met the 24-year-old 4th Duke of Gordon, who was captivated by her beauty and spirit, and they were soon married. Shortly afterwards she received a letter from abroad in a well-known hand: the soldier was alive and well and anxious to marry her. She was distraught, fled the house and was later found stretched out by a burn in a highly emotional state.

Despite its fecundity in terms of children who were to provide genetic material for the senior echelons of the aristocracy and in the late 20th century for the House of Windsor, the marriage of Jane and Alexander was an abject failure in other respects and in the end she moved out of Gordon Castle to a house at Kinrara. Earlier Jane had taken to a life of gaiety, excitement and vanity. She became famous as a leader of fashion and for the brilliance of her assemblies, which were attended by the outstanding wits, orators, poets and statesmen of the day. Her lavish style was not to the Duke's liking, and by about 1790 he had established a strong relationship with Jean Christie—a union which was always supremely happy.

It is apparent that Jean Christie was the light of Alexander's life, and he eventually married her, in 1820, eight years after Jane's death. Among the poems he addressed to her is one beginning:

> Come, come, dear Jean since winter's chill
> And ilka wreath o' snows awa
> We'll lea the Town and to the hill
> An' kye and sheep will ca'
>
> Fae up among Glenfiddich's braes
> Aneath some birkin tree
> A couthy shieling I will raise
> To hand my love to me.

Letters written by Jane Maxwell in 1804 and 1805 (7) reveal that she had developed an overwhelming bitterness towards her husband.

She had accepted 'The Duke's George', who was born before her marriage, but she was infuriated by Alexander's subsequent association with Jean Christie and their procreative activities. She could describe him in 1805, eighteen years after their wedding, as 'a man void of every generous principle' and refer to 'the depravity of the Gordon Castle family' (7). The marital disagreements were not confined to questions of infidelity. It is evident that financial matters were also a source of conflict, Alexander complaining of Jane's extravagant entertaining, and she of his alleged meanness, charging also that the Factors would hide their mismanagement of the estates under 'sums given to the Duchess' (7). As early as 1792 she had been proposing to build a 'shieling' (house) at Badenoch, and she eventually occupied an old farmhouse at Kinrara where she spent an increasing proportion of her time as the years passed. Around 1802 the Duke built a new home for her, Kinrara House, in a lovely situation close to the Spey (7).

Jane Maxwell had a serious side to her character. She was intelligent and well read, and corresponded with Hume, Scott, Burns and others prominent in literature. Burns described her as 'witty and sensible', and in a letter dated 1786 he listed her first among his patrons (28). He also wrote of her husband 'The Duke makes me happier than ever great man did'(7), a somewhat curious statement reflecting the inverted criteria of greatness of the times. David Daiches (28) wrote 'The beautiful and brilliant Duchess of Gordon graced the rustic poet with her social approval—this was tantamount to giving him the entree to Edinburgh society'.

Jane's best friend was Professor James Beattie of Aberdeen, a philosopher and poet.In reviewing a book by Veitch on Scottish poetry, Oscar Wilde stated that Beattie 'approached the problems that Wordsworth afterwards solved'. Whether the relationship between Jane and Beattie transcended mere friendship is not clear. On his death she wrote 'I flatter myself now he sees with what friendship and respect and adoration I valued him in life', and, to Beattie's successor, 'I feel a pleasure in conversing with one who knew Dr. Beattie, loved him as I do, and, indeed, soothed the last moment of a long, long-lingering illness' (7). George Gordon thought (7) that 'since the physical appearance of the worthy professor—slouching gait and gloomy countenance—was hardly likely to kindle the fire of romance within the breast of the handsomest woman in the land, we must conclude that the attraction lay wholly in the realm of the intellect'. However he quotes from a letter from Jane to Beattie, written in 1792: 'Your society for many years made the joy of my life', and 'How I should like to spend some days with you and have one more walk upon the solitary shore where we used to be so gay and happy'.

Jane had great powers of persuasion, which she often put to good effect on behalf of her friends or in pursuit of her own ends. She was highly successful in marrying off her daughters to men of high rank in the dubious scale of the aristocracy. However there were some notable failures. She had plans for a union between Charlotte and Pitt the Younger, but the young Prime Minister, brilliant politician as he was, eluded her match-making intrigues. He remained however, her favourite politician, referred to as 'dear, dear Mr. Pitt' (7). Another failure was her attempt, on a visit to Paris during a break in the Napoleonic wars, to marry her daughter Georgina to Napoleon's stepson, Eugène, the son of Josephine and the Vicomte de Beauharnais. However Bonaparte contemplated a higher alliance for Eugène. As in the Pitt affair, Jane harboured no resentment and 'openly declared that she hoped to see General Bonaparte breakfast in Ireland, dine in England and sup at Gordon Castle'(7). On her return to England the Countess of Errol suggested that she should be sent to the Tower.

The Duchess had other enemies and detractors, among them the 7th Earl of Findlater and Seaford, a neighbour of the Gordons. On one occasion, George Gordon recounts (7), the Brodie of Brodie was describing to Findlater the launching of a new vessel, The Duchess of Gordon, emphasizing that a novel feature of the ship was a copper bottom on which she could rest high and dry at low tide in the Moray ports. Findlater commented 'Weel Brodie, I aye kent that yer Duchess had a brass neck and a brazen face, but I niver kent she had a copper arse.' The remark led to his permanent exile: when the story reached the Duchess she instructed her lawyers to move against the Earl in the

House of Lords, whereupon to avoid the action he escaped to his estates in Germany, never to return to Scotland.

The extent of Jane Maxwell's direct influence on Georgiana is obscure. Although Jane eventually had forty grandchildren, Georgiana was the elder daughter of her favourite child, George, and would presumably have merited some attention. However Georgiana was only eight when Jane died, and it is doubtful whether they ever lived in the same house. Georgiana appears to have inherited much of Jane's spirit, perhaps a little more indomitable and a little less blythe, but blended with creative talents that Jane never displayed. The old Duke, Alexander, probably had more direct influence in moulding Georgiana's character during her visits to Gordon Castle, but later during the years she lived there she was already grown up and he in his old age.

Alexander died in 1828. George Gordon (7) wrote 'With the death of Alexander, 4th Duke of Gordon, the North of Scotland lost one of its great personalities; for over seventy years—the space of three generations—he had reigned as head of this great family and its vast possessions; in power, in wealth, or in influence, there were few in Scotland to compare with him. It was, truly, the end of an era.'

Georgiana's father, the 8th Marquis of Huntly, was born in Edinburgh in 1770, and spent his early boyhood at Gordon Castle, largely in the company of his elder half-brother, the other George. Later he went to Eton and then to St. John's College, Cambridge. His mother wrote to Beattie that he seemed very happy and had talents for everything, adding 'College will determine if he has application, which I am more doubtful of' (7). He eventually embarked on a military career, raising a company for the Black Watch in 1790, and becoming its commander. In 1792 he received a commission in the Scots Guards and early in 1793 all three Guards regiments—Grenadiers, Coldstream and Scots—left for active service in Holland. After participating in the campaign against the French, Huntly returned to Britain and was involved in negotiations to raise a new regiment—the 100th Regiment of Foot, or Gordon Highlanders. In 1796 he became its Colonel while serving in Corsica, which had just seceded from France. Returning to England, his ship was captured in the

Bay of Biscay by a French privateer. He and a number of other British subjects were taken to Bordeaux and stripped of their possessions, but released on condition that a similar number of French prisoners would be returned in exchange (7).

In 1796 or 1797 the Marquis began a long-running relationship with Ann Thomson, who bore him two children: in 1798 Charles, and in 1805 Susan. George Gordon writes (7) that for a dozen years Ann was the prime object of the Marquis' affections, but makes no mention of either Jane Graham or Georgiana, who was born in 1804. It has been suggested that this omission may be because Georgiana was born in London, but we find this explanation somewhat unsatisfying. Georgiana's long years of residence at Gordon Castle, her marriage there, and the records she would have left, including her portraits and other works of art, suggest that her existence would have been evident to any chronicler, unless a deliberate attempt had been made to expunge her from the official Gordon records. As we shall see, the person most likely to have a motive for doing this is Elizabeth Brodie, wife of the 5th Duke, whom he married in 1813.

Like his mother, Huntly seems to have been an extremely convivial type of person, and his rapid promotion in the army may have been the consequence of a combination of his way of getting on well with people of all stations from the King to men of the line, of his connections within the ruling class and probably of some innate abilities, although of these we have only limited concrete evidence. In this respect he differs from his father and his daughter Georgiana, both of whom left ample evidence of their talents.

In 1798 the Gordon Highlanders were transferred to Ireland to help thwart Napoleon's idea of exploiting the Irish push for independence and using the country itself as a springboard for the invasion of England. Huntly was promoted to Brigadier. The Gordons built up an excellent reputation in their treatment of the peasants in Wexford, prompting Sir John Moore to write: 'the good conduct of the 100th Regiment to the people and the affable manners of Lord Huntly did much to reconcile them and bring them back to their habitations'(7).In the same year the regiment was renumbered and became known as the 92nd or Gordon Highlanders. They did not see action against the French in Ireland, and in 1799 they were posted to Holland. The Marquis was seriously wounded in the shoulder at the battle of Egmont-op-Zee, and the fragmented bullet was not removed until a very painful operation, borne with fortitude, was performed in 1806.

Huntly's military career continued to prosper, as recounted by George Gordon (7). He was appointed Colonel of the Black Watch on an order from the King, but he was privately to regret leaving the Gordon Highlanders, and was even accused of disloyalty. He was promoted to Lt-General in 1806, and much later on the death of the Duke of Gloucester in 1835 he became Colonel of the Scots Guards (then known as the Scots Fusilier Guards). In 1808 he was made Lord Lieutenant of Aberdeenshire, and later he was offered several colonial governorships: Canada, in 1827, and Jamaica in 1828. The King said he should have preferred him for India, but that Jamaica was open (following the return to England of Huntly's brother-in-law, the Duke of Manchester). Huntly refused these offers, apparently without offending the King. He was much engaged at the time in rebuilding a part of Gordon Castle which had been destroyed by fire shortly after his father's death in 1827, when he had become the 5th Duke of Gordon. Much earlier Peel had spoken of him as the ideal successor to the Duke of Richmond as Lord Lieutenant of Ireland. Between 1798 and 1807 this post had been occupied by two of his brothers-in-law, Bedford and Richmond, and by his sister's father-in-law, Cornwallis.

In 1813 the Marquis married Elizabeth Brodie, 24 years his junior and from an immensely rich family. Elizabeth was a devout woman and seems to have enjoyed an amiable relationship with her husband, and even, in the end, to have curbed his somewhat irreligious ways. She performed many good works, such as the establishment of the Gordon Schools at Huntly, in Aberdeenshire. However, for those who understand her relationship to Georgiana a very black cloud will always hang over her name. This relationship has been explored by Niall (2), who provides full details of Elizabeth's defalcations, while showing some sympathetic understanding of the circumstances which determined her attitude.

In April 1836 the Duke became seriously ill in London and died on 28th May, the cause of death, revealed by a post-mortem examination, being stomach cancer (7). His will, in which provision was made for Georgiana, was unsigned. The Duchess never honoured his intention. She died in 1864 and even then her promises were not fulfilled, much to Georgiana's surprise and disappointment. It appears that the Duchess adopted a somewhat ambivalent attitude towards Georgiana, to put it charitably. She addressed her in affectionate terms, as shown, for example, by a letter in our possession; on the other hand she cut her out of her inheritance.

Much earlier the young Georgiana had fallen in love with a distant cousin, Peter Charles (known as Perico) Gordon, one of the Catholic Wardhouse Gordons, who lived with his uncle in Spain. The romance had been ended by the Duchess, on sectarian grounds, perhaps blended with malice (29). Brenda Niall (2) has given a slightly abridged version of Georgiana's account of this affair, taken from a manucript entitled 'Stray Leaves from an old Journal long since committed to the flames'.

Why the Duke's will was unsigned is an intriguing question. It is rumoured that a will drawn up by the Duke in the form of a leatherbound book, every page signed by a notary public named Kilgour, and with Georgiana as a main beneficiary, is held by descendants in Sydney. However we have not seen this document, and are unable to confirm its existence. An examination of the Duke's movements in the weeks before his death, as recounted in George Gordon's book (7) leads to a plausible reason for his not signing the will. The Duke and Duchess left Gordon Castle for London in March 1836, and he became seriously ill in London in the middle of April. He died on 28th May without leaving London. He could well have left instructions for drawing up the will as he passed through Edinburgh, intending to sign the document on his return.

Reference to her father in Georgiana's summary of the Gordon family history (in manuscript) is confined to a brief statement of the

Gordon Castle
Dec. 2d 1833.

My dearest Georgiana

My letters to you
are always filled with
pleasure &. I will not make
any, but I must say
I never have been so
nearly overwhelmed
with Company as this
Year as they have all
been off in two day last.
To whom I am obliged to
devote myself for a Great
while...

Letter from Elizabeth Brodie, Duchess of Gordon, to Georgiana

dates of his birth, marriage and death, and that his wife Elizabeth was the daughter of James Brodie of Ayr Hall, that he was a General in the Army, Governor of Edinburgh Castle and K.C.G., that he had no legitimate issue and that his nephew Charles, Duke of Richmond succeeded to the Estates. Georgiana's relations with her father appear to have been good, if not close. He wrote to her affectionately, and gave her gifts (2) and clearly intended that she should be provided for after his death. However he was derelict in making such provision conditional on his widow's goodwill, which was not to be forthcoming. The extent to which Georgiana was deprived of her expectations can be gauged from an inspection of a Disposition relating to the estate of Georgiana's uncle, Adam Gordon, a son of Alexander, the 4th Duke, and Jean Christie.

Adam had promised to divide his estate of Newton Garioch between Georgiana and her half-brother Charles, and had written a will to this effect. However, when he died in 1834 in only his thirtyseventh year, the will was unsigned (as was that of his half-brother George, the 5th Duke, who died two years later). In the absence of a valid will the estate passed to George, who signed a Disposition on February 28th 1835 in favour of 'Eliza, Duchess of Gordon, whom failing to Charles Gordon Esquire Captain in the Royal Navy and Georgina (*sic*) Gordon wife of Andrew McCrae Esquire Solicitor in London and the respective heirs and successors of the said Charles Gordon & Georgina Gordon equally between them share and share alike heritably and irredeemably…' There follows a list of towns, lands, houses, orchards, parks and fairs. These were to be disposed of as indicated above, 'Together with the whole Tolls Customs emoluments profits and duties belonging or by the laws and practice of this Kingdom are known to belong to be Collected and levied by the said Eliza Duchess of Gordon Whom Failing as aforesaid…' If the words 'whom failing' mean 'upon whose death' the magnitude of Elizabeth's defalcation becomes apparent. The disposition was not conditional upon her whim, or upon Georgiana's and Charles' legitimacy. Several other references to Eliza are followed by the phrase 'by whom failing as aforesaid'. However the matter was clouded to some extent by a codicil expressing the hope that the Duchess would not forget his daughter Susan.

Religious Affiliations of the Gordons

As shown by several entries in this notebook, the young Georgiana showed a high degree of piety, and it may be relevant to mention the changing religious affiliations of the Gordons. At one time they were the leading Catholic family in the north-east of Scotland. The Catholic connection was not always smooth. 'Bishop David Stewart, who succeeded to the see of Elgin in 1461, excommunicated the 1st Earl of Huntly for resisting payment of rents. Irritated by this, the Earl threatened to pluck the bishop out of his pigeon-holes in scorn of the mean dwelling at Spyvie at that date. But the haughty prelate, who was rebuilding, rejoined that he should by and by have a nest that the Earl and all his clan should not be able to pluck him out of and the great tower at Spyvie Palace known as 'Davy's' tower, although much shattered today, survives to show that the Bishop's reply was no empty boast'(30).

And later: 'The last public celebration of Mass within the Cathedral took place a whole generation after the Papal authority had been proscribed. After the Battle of Glenlivet on 4th October, 1594, when the leaders of the Catholic forces, the Earls of Huntly and Errol, had defeated the Government forces under Argyle, the party realized that it had no outside support. The Earls and their adherents... assembled within the Cathedral at Elgin to discuss the situation. After Mass had been celebrated James Gordon, a Jesuit priest and uncle to Huntly, descended from the high altar and from the steps of the chancel implored his kinsmen and friends to remain in their own land and hazard all for their faith. It was in vain. The spirit of the Gordons and Hays was broken and early in 1595 Errol embarked at Peterhead for the Continent, as did Huntly at Aberdeen' (30). Later the Gordons traditionally supported the Stewarts and were involved in three of the four attempts by the Jacobites to secure the throne. The 6th Earl of Huntly was converted from Catholicism to the Church of England,

Interior sketch by Georgiana, probably of the room
in which most of the book was written

but was excommunicated on suspicion of receiving and protecting Jesuits
in his castle (10), whereupon the family apparently reverted to the Catholic
faith.

In 1720 Alexander, the 2nd Duke of Gordon, named his son Cosmo
in honour of his friendship with the Catholic Cosmo de Medici III, Grand
Duke of Tuscany, a member of the once powerful Florentine family (7).
On Alexander's deathbed he extracted a promise from his wife the
protestant Henrietta Mordaunt, to bring up their children as Catholics.
However on the first Sunday after his death she took them to the nearest
Protestant (Episcopal) church. In a strange irony a descendant of Alexander,
Cosmo Gordon Lang, became Archbishop of Canterbury in the 20th
century. Henrietta's grandson, George, was the leader of the Gordon riots,
'the most formidable popular rising of the eighteenth century' (10), which
were directed initially against the Catholic Relief Act but soon became a
violent crusade against Catholics and the Catholic Church. Lord George,
M.P. for Luggershall and President of the Protestant Association, had a

parliamentary reputation for making biting but eccentric interventions; he 'firmly believed that he was commissioned from on High to exterminate the papists—which work he set about *con furore'*. Eventually Gordon himself saw that the riots were proceeding too violently and disavowed his old friends, but soldiers shot 200 people dead and many more were wounded, while 135 rioters were arrested and 21 executed. The riots were described by Dickens in 'Barnaby Rudge'. Lord George was tried for High Treason but escaped execution. He was, however, sentenced in 1787 for a libel on Marie Antoinette to imprisonment in Newgate—where he was found dead in his bed on the eve of the expiry of his sentence ('not without suspicion of poison'). He is reputed to have became a convert to Judaism (10).

The family remained Protestant. It is recorded that the 4th Duke of Gordon was interred in Elgin Cathedral on 24th July 1827, after a service conducted by a clergyman of the Scottish Episcopal Church. Elizabeth Brodie, widow of the 5th Duke, became more and more religious; she eventually espoused the Free Church cause and became a Presbyterian. In

The ruins of Elgin Cathedral

Elgin Cathedral: the Gordon tombs

1846 she wrote in a letter 'Had it been said to me at one time that I should become a Presbyterian and a Dissenter I should have replied, 'Is thy servant a dog to do this thing?" (7). Her decision did not have much effect on the Gordons as a family because she had no children and by this time her late husband's illegitimate offspring were approaching middle age. Georgiana and her immediate descendants described themselves as Church of England, but oddly enough her daughter Frances embraced Catholicism at one stage of her life. Most of Georgiana's later descendants are now either Anglican or non-religious.

The Grahams

In contrast to the copious records of the Gordons, information is relatively sparse on Georgiana's maternal antecedents. Her mother, Jane, who lived from 1772 to 1838, was the daughter of Ralph Graham and his wife Margaret Ditchburn, who was the only child of William Ditchburn Esquire of Denwick, Co. Northumberland and his wife Jane Strachan of Brancepeth, Co. Northumberland. Ralph's father, described in family records as Ralph Graham of Rockmoor, near Howick, Co.

Northumberland, had married Dorothy (widow of Robert Hall, M.D., of Newcastle upon Tyne, and founder of the Baths there), who bore him eight children.

In order to understand Georgiana's place in society more fully it is instructive to study her antecedents on both sides. It is romantically tempting to accept Brenda Niall's assessment (2) that there was nothing middle class about Georgiana—that she was the product of the unskilled proletariat and the bluest-blooded aristocracy. This was based on the fact that Ralph Graham gave his occupation as labourer in baptismal records for Jane Graham's older brothers and sisters (2) and that the Northumberland County Council archives contain no reference to Rockmoor. The possibility thus arose that Jane Graham gave her daughter a gentrified account of her background, at least on the paternal side. The younger Ralph who, according to the family records, may have worked on his father's farm, succeeded to the elusive Rockmoor, and apparently gambled away the fortune which his wife Margaret had inherited in the form of the properties of two bachelor uncles 'landed and funded to the amount of 15.000 pounds'. However it is recorded that at some stage Ralph purchased a house in Alnwick.

Ralph Graham's eldest brother Joseph sailed with Anson in 1774. Another elder brother, Robert Graham, 'who held the farm of Lesbury', emigrated in 1788 to Charleston, South Carolina, and a sister, Elizabeth, married Robert Carr, an attorney at Berwick on Tweed.

Of the children of Ralph and Margaret, the eldest, William, went to Bengal as a ship and boat builder, and married Miss Spink, daughter of the head of the firm. William later retired from shipbuilding and settled at Benares, where he had extensive indigo grounds. Dorothy died of whooping cough, aged three. Elizabeth married William Wood Esq. of Etal Mills in Northumberland. Another Dorothy married Thomas Clerk of Windsor, Berkshire. Margaret died unmarried 'bequeathing to her sister Jane and me all her means' (Georgiana was then nine). Another Ralph was killed at the age of 23 years by a fall from a coconut tree at the Isle of St. Helena, where he had put in on his voyage out to Calcutta to act as Foreman in the building yard of Spink & Co.

Thus it appears that Georgiana was not quite as far removed from the hereditary influence of the middle class as her biographer implies (2), but it is probably true that she was essentially a classless individual, equally at home with people from any background or race.

Hugh McCrae mentions an aunt in his rendering of Georgiana's memoirs of her childhood (3). Georgiana remembered attending her funeral in the rain, and an old man remarking: 'Tis no such hurt, this weather, to be dead'. After the ceremony Georgiana and her mother went to the aunt's house 'and saw crushed rosemary leaves mixed with footmarks where the coffin had been borne.' In trying to pass over these, Georgiana's limbs gave way, and she sank unconscious to the floor (3).

Jane Graham is mentioned several times in 'Georgiana in England', but never with any clear depiction of her appearance, behaviour or character. When Georgiana was nine she was laid up with an injured leg for several weeks, during which, she recalled later, 'my mother condescended to beggar me at cards'. The use of the word 'condescended' is unusual in this context, and may be significant. We have no exact indication of when Jane met with the accident which 'affected her at times', but Caroline Clemente (2) believes it must have been after the 1826 portrait by Hawkins, reproduced in colour in Georgiana's biography, and sensitively described in the Catalogue of the Plates. At the age of 54, and 22 years after Georgiana's birth, Jane is portrayed as a woman of handsome and youthful appearance; there is an unmistakable resemblance between the faces of Jane and Georgiana, both of which display character and firmness of purpose.

Australia

Georgiana's life in Australia has been well documented, particularly in her own Journal (1) and in her biography (2). She arrived in the infant colony of Port Phillip, then part of New South Wales, in the barque 'Argyle' on 1st March 1841 and spent nearly half a century in Melbourne, except for the years 1845 to 1851, when she lived at 'Arthur's Seat on the bay of Port Phillip' as she described it. The family were pioneers on the Mornington Peninsula, a stretch of land south of

Melbourne enclosed by the coastline of Port Phillip Bay, Bass Strait, and Westernport Bay and a line joining what are now the towns of Frankston and Hastings.

Five children were born to Andrew and Georgiana McCrae before they left Britain. The first, Elizabeth Margaret, born on 14th September 1831 was baptized at Edinburgh on 2nd December, and died in Westminster on 13th June 1834. Georgiana's grief is reflected in various entries in this volume. A delicate pencil sketch of her daughter, dated 10th June 1834 and stained by the artist's tears, has been described as one of the saddest drawings in Australian history, in the mistaken belief that the subject was Agnes, the McCraes' youngest child. However it is clear from the date that the drawing was of Elizabeth, and was made well before Georgiana came to Australia.

The next four children were sons:

George Gordon, b. 29th May 1833, baptized Edinburgh 10th September 1833

William Gordon, b. 1st March 1835, bapt. Edinburgh 24th March 1835

Alexander Gordon, b. 30th November 1836, bapt. Edinburgh 13th January 1837

Farquhar Peregrine, b. 7th September 1837 at Milton, Gravesend, bapt. Gravesend 4th November 1837.

All the Australians in the family were daughters:

Georgiana Lucia, b. 29th December 1841 at Melbourne, bapt. St. James Church 30th January 1842

Margaret Martha, b. 25th June 1844 at 'Mayfield' (the McCrae house, later demolished to make way for a factory, situated in what is now the Melbourne suburb of Collingwood), bapt. Mayfield 7th August 1844

Octavia Frances Gordon, b. 20th June, 1847 at Arthur's Seat, bapt. Melbourne 29th October, 1847

Agnes Thomasine Gordon, b. 27th March 1851 at Arthur's Seat, died Melbourne, 10th January 1854.

Above: William Gordon McCrae, Georgiana's second son (left);
Alexander Gordon McCrae, her third son (right). *Below:* A copy by
Barbara Blomfield of Georgiana's sketch of Elizabeth, her infant
daughter (left); Lucia Hyndman, another daughter (right)

Like her sister Elizabeth 22 years earlier, Agnes was not yet three years old when she died. Frances later described the occasion thus (6): 'The baby of the house sickened, and after an attack of measles water on the brain followed, and the little one gradually faded away, much to the grief of her sisters and brothers, and for the father and mother it was a terrible sorrow.' On this second tragic occasion in her life Georgiana wrote in the family bible:

> Ere sin could blight or sorrow fade
> Death came with friendly care
> The opening bud to heav'n conveyed
> And bade it blossom there.

The formal part of her diary as published (1) ends in August 1845, with only sporadic contributions over the ensuing years, labelled 'scrip-scrap' by her Editor, Hugh McCrae. No reference can be found to Agnes' death.

The McCraes

Georgiana's husband, Andrew Murison McCrae was a distant relative of the Gordons. According to family records his great great grandfather Alexander Macrae (as it was then spelt) married Agnes Gordon, daughter of Gordon of Carleton, a cadet of Earlston, of the Kenmure family, who in his turn was a cadet of William de Stitchele, third son of the Earl of Huntly. With Agnes Gordon he had the property of Glenlair (spelt Glenlayer in Georgiana's account) in the parish of Parton in the Stewartry of Kircudbright as her dower. In earlier times the Macraes had been the traditional custodians of Castle Eilean Donan, on Loch Duich, Wester Ross, a stronghold of the Mackenzies built originally in the 13th century.

Alexander's son, also Alexander, born at Glenlair in 1745, went to Jamaica as a young man to be employed on the estate of the Honourable William Harvie, whose sister Mary he married in 1767. Mary's father, Thomas Harvie, has been variously described as Town Clerk of Glasgow and sometime Rector of the Grammar School, Glasgow. William Harvie was a Member of Assembly and Assistant Judge of the Grand Court of Jamaica. Alexander's fortunes prospered on the basis of cheap slave labour and he became the owner of several sugar plantations. He owned many slaves and became known as 'The Nabob.' William Gordon Macrae, son of Alexander and Mary, was born at Belle Isle near Ayr in 1768. His mother died in Jamaica in 1770 and William lived until he was seven years old with his uncle, William Harvie, who then sent him to school in England, first at

Andrew Murison McCrae, by Georgiana McCrae, c.1830
State Library of Victoria

Newcastle-upon-Tyne and afterwards at Westminster School and King's College, Aberdeenshire. He served his time in the house of Myers and McGlashan, Attorneys, and then went to live with his father in Jamaica. It is recorded that he was 'a Whig from principle' and 'a hater of oppression in every shape, and soon became known as the friend and advocate of the negroes, defending them as opportunity required.' He was a supporter of Wilberforce, and, according to family records prepared by Frances Moore (McCrae) he liberated all his slaves when his father died and being unable to work his estates without them he left his property in the West Indies as a matter of conscience and went back to Scotland. He farmed for a time at Westbrook and then obtained a minor position in the Customs House. He changed his name from Macrae to McCrae, evidently to dissociate himself more completely from his father's slave-owning activities. He became known as 'The Liberator'. A slightly different account, which is probably correct since it was written by his son Andrew, suggests that William was disinherited by his father for his abolitionist views. Brenda Niall (2) is not convinced that William took an active part in the anti-slavery movement, because this is not claimed in several other accounts of his father written by Andrew McCrae. However if his father disinherited him for his support of the cause of the slaves, it would seem to imply that he was active in this area.

Sir Alexander Morison, M.D., uncle of Andrew McCrae

In 1796 William married Margaret Murison, only daughter of Andrew Murison of Anchorfield and Hetland, near Dumfries. The names Murison and Morison were apparently interchangeable; a brother of Margaret, Sir Alexander Morison, M.D., ('dear Uncle Sandy' to Georgiana), President of the Royal College of Physicians in Edinburgh, was well known for his treatment of mental disorders (2). He was also physician to the unfortunate Princess Charlotte, who died in childbirth at the age of twenty.

The McCraes had eight children, including Andrew Murison McCrae, born in 1800, who became a Writer to the Signet in Edinburgh and married Georgiana at Gordon Castle, Fochabers in 1830. In addition to Andrew and Georgiana, Andrew's two brothers, Alexander (b. 1799) and Farquhar (b. 1806), and his three sisters Mary Harvie (b. 1797), Thomas Ann (b. 1810) and Margaret (b. 1812) emigrated to Port Phillip.

William McCrae's humanitarian principles and anti-racist activities clearly influenced the attitudes of his children and other descendants towards the indigenous peoples of Australia and New Zealand. His eldest son, Alexander, while an Ensign of the 8th Regiment (York and Lancaster) in New Zealand in 1820, kept a Journal, which was later edited by Sir Frederick Chapman and published in 1928 (31). The young officer showed a deep appreciation of the cultural values of the Maoris, and of their ability. Commenting on an incident in which one of the early missionaries had been driven away by the natives, Alexander remarked that it was 'solely in consequence of his having interfered with them in matters he had no business with', adding that 'nothing is more foolish and dangerous than to violate the customs of any people.' And again: 'Their physiognomy is very prepossessing, and marks distinctly the natural acuteness of their understanding and the sensibility of their nature.'... The Maoris 'displayed a surprising dexterity in the use of our tools which was a sufficient indication to us how rapidly they would advance in the arts of civilized life were opportunities afforded for the development of their capacities.' McCrae is generous in his praise of his hosts in New Zealand: 'Among no people are the duties of Hospitality better known or practised. They have been accused of treachery and cruelty, but certainly without sufficient reason. I myself found them to be unsuspecting, friendly and humane, and though much in their power in my various excursions felt as secure amongst them as in my Native Country, and certainly more so than I have done in some countries boasting the advantages of Civilization.' These sentiments strongly reminded one of us (H.G.H.) of impressions formed and recorded during various excursions in New Guinea nearly sixty years ago.

Alexander McCrae was close to his brother Andrew and sister-in-law Georgiana before they left Scotland and later in Australia. In the new colony he became Postmaster-General in the first Victorian Government. A grandson, the late Maurice Blackburn, was a lawyer and independent politician renowned for his humanitarian and progressive liberal attitudes. Two of Maurice's sons are successful scientists and a daughter-in-law is well known for the 'Blackburn Report', which has had a profound, if controversial effect on secondary education in Victoria.

Carrick-on-Suir
23 Apl 1840

My dear Georgiana

With your letter I rec'd this morning a paper from I am (the Port Phillip Patriot) containing the address to the Lt. Governor. with his answer &c. It is really most unaccountable that no one has written considering how anxious they must know would be to hear from them. This paper seems to have come by the common course of post, without the P charge. I see an advertisement of Mr Dr. W. announcing that he intends to practise as a solicitor & conveyancer in Melbourne as soon as he shall have rec'd the necessary permission from the Supreme Court at Sydney, and in an acc't of sales of land near Melbourne I find Farquhars name down as the purchaser of two lots one of 315 acres price £844. another of 323 acres price £1227. These lots were bought at a late sale and must be in addition to what he bought by himself

Letter from Alexander McCrae to Georgiana

Andrew McCrae was on friendly terms with members of the Bunurong tribe of Aborigines, with whom he had constant dealings on his property on the Mornington Peninsula. Georgiana was a friend to them all, tended to their wants and drew their portraits with the same understanding, compassion and respect she had earlier shown in the representation of Scottish aristocrats. She had also been interested in linguistics, as shown by several entries in this book, and she and her son George made a serious attempt to learn the Bunurong language (2). The Aborigines would squat on the verandah of the homestead and listen to her playing lively Scottish airs, which delighted them exceedingly, as they showed their admiration with loud cries, waving hands and keeping time with the music (6). His parents' regard for the Aborigines was transmitted to the young George McCrae and was a theme which came through strongly in his literary work.

Andrew's younger brother, Farquhar, a doctor, was well known in early Melbourne (1, 2, 32), and was much more entrepreneurial than his brothers. In addition to his medical activities he was a substantial landowner in Melbourne and in the countryside. In 1839 he took over a station where the town of Dandenong now stands, as well as the adjoining one, Eumemmering. A 'Plan of the Town of Melbourne' published by John Pascoe Fawkner in 1841 shows Dr. McCrae as the owner of large blocks in Hoddle Street, on the corner of Simpson's Road (now Victoria Street) and on the corner of Bridge Road (1). Punts operated across the southern end of Elizabeth Street and also of Hoddle Street, the continuation of which to the south thus becoming known as Punt Road. Exhibition Street is shown on the plan by its original name of Stephen Street.

Farquhar's name is sometimes mentioned (1) in connection with the first use of chloroform as an anaesthetic in Victoria, but it appears that his brother-in-law Dr. David John Thomas, the first surgeon of the Melbourne (now Royal Melbourne) Hospital may have been the real pioneer of anaesthesia in the colony, in using ether for amputations and in the removal of tumors. This was in 1847, the same year in which Professor James Simpson, in Glasgow, was pioneering the use of

Left: Dr. David Thomas, brother-in-law of Andrew McCrae;
Right: Mrs. Margaret Thomas, sister of Andrew McCrae

chloroform in surgery. Simpson incidentally, was the husband of Farquhar McCrae's niece, the daughter of his sister Agnes, who had married William Stuart Bruce of the Island of Whalesey in the Shetlands. (The Island had been given to an ancestor of Bruce by Mary Queen of Scots, and the deed of gift with her signature is carefully preserved by the family.)

Thus Farquhar would have had access to information on anaesthesia from two close family sources, and he was certainly an early practitioner of the new technique. Georgiana records that a Dr. Owen, who arrived at Port Phillip from Sydney in 1843 with a letter of introduction had known Farquhar and William Bruce in Edinburgh, and Simpson would have moved in the same circles. One of the earliest portraits hanging in the gallery of the Royal Australasian College of Surgeons in Melbourne is that of Farquhar, painted by Georgiana. Farquhar served as an army surgeon, and his sword is also on display.

However the early social and economic successes of Farquhar McCrae were not to continue. He later ran into financial difficulties, quarrelled with his brother Andrew and with J.L.Foster, to whom he had sold the lease of the Eumemmerring run (2), and eventually moved to Sydney.

Dr. Thomas, a Welshman, had married Farquhar's sister Margaret in Melbourne in 1840. When Georgiana moved from Melbourne to Arthur's Seat one of her main causes for lament was the distance from Dr. Thomas and his medical skills.

The character of Andrew Murison McCrae has tended to be obscured by the attention which historians, art critics and various authors have devoted to his wife, and his character has even been misrepresented by certain authors and journalists. In fact Andrew has been as consistently vilified as Georgiana has been exalted. Brenda Niall has succeeded in putting Andrew into proper perspective (2), but a little more remains to be done to complete the rehabilitation. His daughter Frances regarded him as noble and unselfish, and his daughter-in-law Augusta, George's wife, described him as an 'old angel'. The bare facts of his life in Australia are that he went into practice in 1839 as a solicitor in Melbourne with James Montgomery, the Clerk of the Peace, as a partner (33). By the end of 1842, however, the economy had collapsed and the partnership, faced with clients who could not honour their debts, was dissolved (29). Andrew decided in 1844 to take up a cattle run at the foot of Arthur's Seat on the Mornington Peninsula, and the family left Melbourne in March 1845. Once again the enterprise was unsuccessful financially, and the McCraes returned to Melbourne in October 1851, the 12 000-acre station being sold for 1000 pounds. With the advent of the gold rush in Victoria, Andrew obtained official positions as Stipendiary and Police Magistrate in various centres, including Alberton, Gippsland (1851-54), Barrow's Inn, Hepburn, Creswick and finally for seven years at Kilmore, where he was also Warden of the Goldfields, Deputy Sheriff and Commissioner of Crown Lands, retiring in 1866 (4, 29). Georgiana and the children did not follow him to the goldfields, but remained in Melbourne.

McCrae appears to have been somewhat dour and down-to-earth in the traditional Scottish way. The unpublished manuscript of a journal written by McCrae in 1845 is in our possession, and has been laboriously transcribed by Jessie Serle. It reveals a man much concerned with practical matters such as the price of wheat and the direction of the prevailing wind, but an enquiring mind is also speculating on the utilization of seaweed in agriculture, whether the high water run-off on his land was fed by springs, whether the native spinach could be used as a substitute for green vegetables and on the possible commercial use of banksia as a cabinet timber. McCrae would read from the 'Cyclopaedia of English Literature' to his friends and from 'Chalmers Astronomical Discoveries' to his sons, noting that 'the boys have a taste for the science'. Byron's works were described as 'immortal breathings'. McCrae played his part in the affairs of the young colony. For example (1) he was one of the sub-committee of three appointed by the Separation Association (the other two being Redmond Barry and J.B. Were), he was Vice-President of the Port Phillip Club (32) and he was the inaugural Secretary of the Australia Felix Pastoral and Agricultural Society (34).

Although Andrew and Georgiana were to found a kind of dynasty, their marriage was not a consistently happy one, and in the end they were living virtually separate lives. For many years it was clear that Andrew harboured a great admiration and affection for his wife, but there is scant evidence of Georgiana's reciprocating these feelings at the same level. On the 14th anniversary of their wedding Andrew wrote a poem for her embellished with lines like 'A form that is faultless for grace and high bearing', 'An eye that expresses the soft and the tender', 'The sweet bird of the magical song' and ending with the words:

> But now to recount all her talents and graces
> The field is too large which the subject embraces
> I shall therefore conclude 'the delight of my life',
> Tho' poorly portrayed—is my true-hearted wife.

Further evidence of his affection for her at this time and concern for her health and welfare is to be found in the unpublished journal, in which Andrew describes his life at Arthur's Seat. However the marriage deteriorated. Georgiana did not accompany him when he took up his posts in country Victoria. In 1867 Andrew left Australia alone to spend seven years in Britain, perhaps a solution to their problems reached by mutual consent (29). He died at Hawthorn on 24th July 1874, soon after his return to Victoria. Georgiana survived him by some sixteen years, dying at Hawthorn on 24th May 1890. They are buried in adjacent graves in Boroondara Cemetery, Kew, near the gate in the wall adjoining Park Hill Road.

Many aspects of Georgiana's life in Australia are well beyond the scope of this brief account of some of the factors which may have determined her character and that of her husband. Primarily, it is hoped that the information presented here may help to put Georgiana's thoughts as a young woman—her tastes, her joys, her sorrows, her beliefs, her fears and her intellectual and creative activities—as expressed in this notebook, into an appropriate social and hereditary context. Her influence has extended to many of her descendants. As regards her life in Australia many fascinating questions remain to be explored and answered.

Georgiana grows on people. Hugh McCrae (16) describes his last visit to his grandmother on his twelfth birthday, on the evening of which she died. She kissed him and gave him a guinea to get a book to remember her by. Soon he began to study her portrait in the drawing-room of his home. He 'read her diaries and looked at her water-colour sketches; learned to love them; to adore her.' Georgiana has had this mysterious effect on others among her descendants, and on a growing number of people to whom she is unrelated. It is hoped that this volume will bring her a little closer to those in our generation who see her as a rather remarkable woman, representing some of the best values of Scottish (and English) culture and able to transplant them and give them new significance in the untilled Australian soil.

Dr. Brenda Niall's biography of Georgiana (2) appeared in 1994, and joins Georgiana's Journal (1) as the main source of information on the life and times of a person who is attracting increasing interest in various roles: as painter, diarist, and pioneer. The product of meticulous research, Niall's biography is written with skill and sensitivity, and displays a high level of psychological insight and scholarship.

In transcribing the notebook we have retained the page breaks of the original (Georgiana's pages were unnumbered), and have made every effort to present the material exactly as it was written, with almost no attempt at correction, even when this might appear to be warranted, at least by modern conventions. The only exceptions to this practice are where very obvious minor errors occur, e.g. in the careless omission of some of the accents in the French passages. Georgiana's handwriting flows easily with a smooth elegance, and is for the most part remarkably clear and legible, although some difficulties in transcription were encountered, mainly with unfamiliar words and phrases. The notebook itself is of good quality, still in excellent condition, coloured red with gold embossing, and with marbling on the front and back linings. The pages are in a variety of pastel shades, which have responded in different ways to the ravages of the years. The front and back of the book are entirely equivalent, which has prompted Georgiana to start her entries at both ends simultaneously. Hence we have the pages labelled simply 'Georgiana Gordon January 1st 1828' on pages 59 and 109 of the present volume, which indicate the two starting points.

The categories used in the list of contents are those of the editors. Georgiana's entries are in chronological order from each end of the book.

Some comments or notes on particular entries are to be found at the end of the book. We have thought it better to put them there than to interrupt the author's thoughts by inserting them in the main body of the text.

Georgiana has not always attributed the entries to their authors, as she had of course no thoughts of publication. Where the authors of such entries are known to us we have inserted them in the list of contents, but not in the text, and have sometimes commented in the notes at the end. In only a few instances will the authorship be still obscure, as Georgiana's own poems are recognizable by the appended date, and the origin of the prose entries is usually evident.

—H.G.H. and B.H.

To Scotland

My native land! my native land!
  How many tender ties,
Connected with thy distant strand
  Call forth my heavy sighs.

The rugged rock — the mountain stream —
  The hoary pine-tree's shade;
Where often, in the noon-tide beam
  A happy child I strayed —!

I think of thee, when early light
  Is trembling on the hill —;
I think of thee at dead midnight
  When all is dark and still!

I think of those whom I shall see
  In this fair earth no more.
And wish in vain for wings to flee
  Back to thy much-loved shore.

Facsimile of a page of the commonplace book

55

References

1. McCrae, G.H. *Georgiana's Journal* (Ed. H. McCrae), Angus and Robertson, Sydney, 1934.

2. Niall, Brenda *Georgiana: A Biography of Georgiana McCrae, Painter, Diarist, Pioneer* Melbourne University Press (1994).

3. McCrae, Hugh 'Southerly' 8(2):89; 8(3):150; 8(4):208 (1947).

4. Cowper, N.L. Introduction to Third Edition of *Georgiana's Journal*, William Brooks, Sydney and Brisbane (1978).

5. Lucas, E.V. *Loiterer's Harvest* Methuen, London (1913).

6. Moore, O.F.G. *The Piano Story*, (1907), printed in 1962 by G.R.Williams, Glen Iris, Victoria.

7. Gordon, G. *The Last Dukes of Gordon and their Consorts 1743-1864*, Taylor and Henderson, Aberdeen (1980).

8. Thompson, F. *Scotland*, Ward Lock, London (1983).

9. Hope, L. *Stars of the Desert*, Heinemann, London.

10. Low, S.J. and Pulling, F.S. (Eds.) *The Dictionary of English History*, Cassell, London (1884).

11. Bellew, J.C.M. *Poet's Corner—A Manual of English Poetry*, Routledge, London (1868).

12. Green, H.M. *A History of Australian Literature*, Angus and Robertson, Sydney (1961).

13. Green, H.M. *Outline of Australian Literature*, Whitcombe and Tombs, Sydney (1930).

14. Miller, E.M. *Australian Literature*, Melbourne University Press (1940); Facsimile Impression Sydney University Press (1973).

15. Healy, J.J. *Literature and the Aborigine in Australia*, University of Queensland Press (1978).

16. McCulloch, A. *Encyclopaedia of Australian Art*, Hutchinson of Australia (1968).

17. McCrae, H. *Story-Book Only*, Angus and Robertson, Sydney (1948).

18. Phillips, A. A. *The Australian Tradition*, Cheshire, Melbourne (1958).

19. *Meanjin* 17(1), No. 72, Autumn, University of Melbourne (1958).

20. Lindsay, N. *The Bulletin*, Sydney, Feb. 26 (1958).

21. Dutton, G. *The Heritage of Australian Poetry*, Currey O'Neil, Melbourne (1976).

22. Palmer, N. **In** *Australian Literature*, L. Kramer and A. Mitchell (Eds), Oxford University Press, Melbourne (1985).

23. Anon. (S) *The Bulletin*, Sydney, April 6 (1949).

24. Simpson, W.D. *Huntly Castle*, H.M. Stationery Office, Edinburgh (1954).

25. Lord Macaulay *The History of England*, Longmans, London (1871).

26. McLeod, D. **In** *A Book of Scotland*, G.F. Maine (Ed.), Collins, London (1950).

27. Campbell, A.H. Personal discussion (1992).

28. Daiches, D. *Robert Burns*, Andre Deutsch, London (1966).

29. Hancock, Marguerite 'Georgiana McCrae', Unpublished thesis, Monash University.

30. Richardson, J.S. and Mackintosh, H.B. *Elgin Cathedral*, H.M. Stationery Office, Edinburgh (1950).

31. McCrae, Alexander **In** *Journal kept in New Zealand in 1820*, F.R. Chapman (Ed.), Government Printer, Wellington (1928).

32. de Serville, P. *Port Phillip Gentlemen*, Oxford University Press (1980).

33. Garryowen (Edmund Finn) *The Chronicles of Early Melbourne 1835 to 1852. Historical, Anecdotal and Personal*, vol. 2, Melbourne (1888).

34. *Port Phillip Herald*, Melbourne, Jan. 17, (1840).

Georgiana Gordon
January 1st 1828

Derivation of Proper names

Abdi, Hebrew - my servant

Abdiah, H - the servant of GOD

Abel, H - vanity

Abiezer, H - the Father's help

Abiathar, H - excellent Father

Abigail, H - the Father's joy

Abner, H - the Father's lamp

Abram or Abraham, - Father of multitudes

Absalom, H - Father's peace

Acamatos, Greek - unwearied

Acantha, Gr - a thorn

Achan, H - troubling

Adam, H - red earth

Adelard, Teutonic - Noble nature

Atheling, Saxon - excellent son

Athelrad, Sax - rare counsel

Agnes, Gr - chaste

Agrippas, Gr - difficult birth

Alan, Slavonian - a wolf dog

Andrew, Gr - manly or courageous

Aletheia, Gr - Truth

Alexander, Gr - helper of men

Amarantha, Gr - everlasting flower

Anthony, Gr - a rosemary flower

Adolphus, Sax - happy help

Adulph, Sax - old help

Augustus or Augustin, Latin - majestic

Auralia, Latin - an airy spirit

Alfred, Sax - all peace

Alice - of noble descent

Adar, H - mighty, also the 12th month corresponding to parts of
    February and March

Alp - a bullfinch
Alphey, Sax - Jack of all trades
Alphonsus - our help
Ambrose, Gr -immortal
Anna, H - Gracious
Ananiah, H - a cloud
Anselus, Teut - defender of his companions
Amos, H - a burden
Amoz - stout and strong
Aaron, H - a mountaineer
Agatha - from the pict word Agathos - good
Amy, French - friendly or kind
Arabella, Lat - a fair altar
Asa, H - a healer of sickness
Archibald, Sax - bold observer
Agelnoth, Sax - void of grief
Aelfagus, Sax - all merry
Aelgiva, Sax - all beautiful
Alianor - all fruitful
Bernard, Sax - stout heart or child of nature
Bernulph, Sax - provider for his children
Beatrix - one that renders happy
Bertha, Sax - brave, famous
Bede - a prayer
Barnabad, H - son of consolation
Belvedera, Italian - pleasant to behold
Bennet, Lat - blessed
Baldwin, Sax - bold conqueror
Baliol - of grief or woeful
Barbara, Lat - foreign or strange
Bartholomew, H - son of the raiser of waters
Brian, H - clamorous
Bartulph, Sax - help in counsel
Barzillai, H - as hard as iron

Basil, Gr - regal or kingly
Berniger, Fr - bearkeeper
Betty, Lat from beatus - blessed
Blanche, Fr - white or fair
Boniface, Italian - a well-doer
Botolph, Sax - boat help, patron of mariners
Bridget, Sax - a little Bride
Caesara, Lat - a cut or gash
Charles, Sax - stout
Cornelius, H - the horse of the sun
Chrysanthe, Gr - from chrysos, gold
Cosmo, Gr - from Cosmos, the world
Cyprian, Lat - a bull rush
Clara, Fr - clear, bright
Charity - natural affection, love
Caiaphat, H - an encompasser
Calliope, Gr - beauty of countenance
Caleb, H - a dog
Canan, H - a merchant
Cadwallader - a captain of war
Carus, Gr - torpid sleep
Clement, Lat - meek, gentle, courteous
Claudian, Lat - shutter or closing
Cordelia, Lat - comfort to the heart
Deborah, H - a bee
Dyonisius, Gr - Bacchus god of wine
Dinah, H - judgement
Doig, H - a careful heraldman
Dousabel, Fr - sweet & fair
Dorabella, Gr - sweet gift
Drosomeli, Gr - honeydew
Dora, Gr - a gift
Dorothy, Gr - God's gift
Daniel, H - the judge of God

David, H - beloved
Dorcas, H - a roe
Dreslie - sorrowful
Edith, Sax - happy & prosperous
Edgar, Sax - happy & honorable
Edwin - obtainer of happiness
Edmund - blessed peace
Egbert - ever flourishing
Eleazar, H - the help of GOD
Elizabeth, Gr - GOD hath sworn
Ella, Sax - valour
Ephraim, H - fruitful
Esau, H - working
Esther, H - secret or hidden
Ethelbald, Sax - nobly bold
Ethelbert, Sax - nobly bright
Ethelfred, Sax - noble peace
Ethelstan, Sax - the noble gem
Ethelward, Sax - noble keeper
Ethelwin, Sax - noble purchaser
Ethelwold, Sax - noble governor
Eugene, Gr - nobly born
Eusebea, Gr - godliness, devotion
Eustace, Gr - standing firm
Eve, H - she lived
Evan, Celtic - John
Erza, H - a helper
Elfrida, Sax - ringlet haired fairy
Enos, H - mortal, sickly, miserable
Euneas, Gr - number nine or ninth
Eglantine, Fr - a wild rose or Aiglentier
Ernest, Sax - earnest
Evander, Lat - fading soon decaying
Eudoxus, Gr - good name

Euphemie, Gr - well spoken of
Eros, Gr - Cupid
Europa, Gr - broadfronted & large eyed
Euphonia, Lat - smooth flowing voice
Ferdinando, Sax - pure peace
Francis - free, careless
Frank, Fr - free, openhearted, generous
Fremund, Sax - free and peaceful
Frederick, Sax - rich peace
Frithwald, Sax - peaceable ruler
Gabriel, H - a mighty one
George, Gr - a husbandman
Gerard, Sax - all nature
German, Sax - studious
Gertrude - true to her trust, or all truth
Gervas - all fast
Gilbert - famous, golden-head
Godard, Sax - compliant disposition
Godfrey, Sax - godlike peace
Godwin, Sax - a conqueror in GOD
Grissel, Fr - a grey lady
Griffith - of great faith
Guy - a leader or banner
Gregory, Gr - watchful
Hagar, H - a stranger
Hadarezer, H - beautiful help
Helena - a healthy one
Hildebert, Sax - famous nobleman
Hilary, Lat - cheerful
Hippocrates, Gr - a mighty horseman
Ham, H - crafty
Harfazer Sax - fairhaired
Hengist - a horse or banner
Henry - honour or rich at home

Hugh, Sax - high or to cleave
Humphrey, Sax - one who makes peace at home
Jacob, H - a supplanter or beguiler
Jack, H - a doe
Jehn, H - being
Jeremiah, H - exalting the Lord
Jesse, H - a graft
Jethro, H - excelling
Joab, H - fatherhood
Joanna, H - the grace of GOD
Job, H - patient
Joriah, H - a dove
Johnathan, H - the gift of God
Joseph, H - increase
Joshua, H - the lord or governour
Josiah, H - the fire of the Lord
Jubal, H - a trumpet
Judah, H - praise
John, H - God's grace
Jill - from Julian or Juliana, a slut
Isaac, H - he shall laugh
Isabella - handsome Elizabeth
Judith, H - praising
Katherine, Gr - pure
Kenred, Sax - bold counsel
Kenric, Sax - valiant ruler
Kenwulph - valiant help
Laban, H - white or shining
Lameck, H - poor or humble
Leah, H - painful
Leander, Sax - concealer
Leonard, Sax - lionhearted
Leonine - belonging to a lion
Leopold, Sax - the people's hold

Lathy, Sax - soft, humble, mild, quiet
Lambert, Sax - a fair lamb
Laetitia, Lat - Joy
Lewis - safeguard of the people
Lionel, Lat - a little lion
Lazarus, H - by the Lord's help
Lot, H - wrapped or joined together
Lucy, Lat - light
Luke, H - indifferent, careless
Lithie, Sax - supple, smooth, languid
Lancelot - a lance or spear
Mabel, Lat - lovely, unaffected
Magdalen - magnified
Malaelis, H - my messenger
Manasseh, H - not forgotten
Margaret, Gr - a pearl
Mary, H - bitterness
Mark - the month of March
Martin, Lat - martial
Matthew, H - a reward
Matthias - the gift of GOD or reward
Maud or Matilda, Sax - a maid
Maximilian - great
Maynard - stout-hearted
Meliscent - honey-sweet
Menahem, H - a comforter
Micajah, H - who is as the Lord?
Michael, H - who is like GOD?
Michal, H - who is perfect?
Minicene, Sax - a nun
Miriam, H - bitterness of affliction
Mordecai, H - bitter
Morgan - born by the seaside
Morice or Morris - dark, obscure

Moses, H - drawn up
Murray, Fr - a mulberry
Naaman, H - comely, fair
Nabal, H - a fool or madman
Nasab, H - a Prince
Nathaniel, H - the gift of GOD
Nehemiah, H - he rested
Noah, H - ceasing or resting
Nicolas, Gr - victorious
Neal, Lat - Nigellus
Obadiah, H - a servant of the Lord
Oliver, Lat - an olive tree
Oreb, H - a crow
Osmund, Sax - house peace
Osborne, Sax - house born
Oswald, Sax - house ruler
Oswy, Sax - consecrated
Olivia - an olive
Paul, Gr - little
Peter, Gr - a Rock or Stone
Pharaoh, H - making bare
Philemon, Gr - a kiss
Philip, Gr - a lover of horses
Patrick, Lat - a senator
Philibert, Sax - very bright
Peregrine, Lat - foreign or outlandish
Phineas - bold countenance
Phillis, Gr - a leaf
Phillirea - an evergreen
Polydora, Gr - liberally gifted
Rachel, H - a sheep
Raphael, H - the healing of God
Ralph, Sax - help, counsel, from Rudolph
Ranulph, Sax - pure help

Raymund, Sax - pure discourse
Reinard, Sax - uncorrupt, honest minded
Rennard - whose honour is untainted
Reuben, H - the son of vision
Robert, Sax - famous counsel
Richard - rich nature, liberal hearted
Roderick, Sax - rich counsel & complexion
Roger, Sax - one desirous of rest
Rosamund, Sax - rosy lipped
Rebecca, H - fat and full
Rowland, Sax - peace maker to his country
Rowena, Sax - to acquire peace
Samuel, H - heard of GOD
Sampson, H - here the second time
Sarah, H - dame or mistress
Senachnib, H - the bramble of destruction
Shibboleth, H - an ear of corn
Sigismund, Sax - one who conquers by good words
Simeon, H - hearing
Solomon, H - peaceable
Sophia, Gr - wisdom
Sophronia, Gr - prudence and temperance
Stephen, Gr - a crown
Susannah, H - a Lily
Tabitha - a roebuck
Theodore, Gr - God's gift
Theobald, Sax - early, virtuous or valiant
Theodrick, Sax - rich people
Theodosia, Gr - the gift of god
Theophilus, Gr - godfriend
Tereza, Italian - the third
Tobiah, H - the goodnes of GOD
Thomas, Gr - doubting or two-hearted
Tubal, H - worldly

Tubaleain, H - the worldly profession
Urban, Lat - courteous, civil
Uriel, H - the fire of the Lord
Ursula - a little she bear
Vaughan - little, small
Vincent - a conqueror or conquering
Walter - a woodranger or pilgrim
Wilfred, Sax - all peace
William, Sax - the defence of many or the wearer of a gilt helmet
Wimund, Sax - sacred peace
Winifred, Sax - to win peace
Waldwin or Walwyn - to rule or Conquer
Walphur, Sax - an helper
Zachariah, H - a memorial
Zimri, H - a song or singing

Christopher, Gr - Christ's Carrier
Dora, Gr - a gift
Prudentia, Lat - wisdom in managing affairs
Ptolemy, Gr - war, or a warrior
Rupert - commander of a troop of horses
Sebastian, Gr - reverend or magisterial
Arthur, Sax - a strong man
Priscilla, Lat - little old woman
Asaph - gathering
James - Spanish of Jacobus
Mildred, Sax - mild in counsel
Herbert, Sax - the glory of an army
Ruthe - pity, compassion
Drusilla, Gr - dewy-eyed
Americk, Sax - always rich
Cuthbert, Sax - known or famed
Drury - sobriety, modesty
Foster - a forester

Franklin - a freeman
Geoffrey, Sax - glad peace
Jerome - holy law

Lines said to be written by Arthur O'Connor
Aberdeen --- 17..

> The Pomps of Courts and pride of Kings
> I prize above all earthly things
> I love my country but the King
> Above all men his praise I sing
> The Royal Banners are display'd
> And may sweep the Standard aid
> I fain would banish far from France
> The right of man & common sense
> Confusion to his adroit reign
> That foe to princes Thomas Paine
> Defeat and ruin seize the cause
> Of France its liberties and laws!

It will easily be perceived that the above lines may be read in three different ways which convey as many meanings.

— — — — — — — —

> Premier, said Fox, I'd have a Tax
>> That should not fall on me.
> That's right, said North then tax <u>Receipts</u>
>> For those you never see.

On the Receipt Tax by ......

72

Derivation of Surnames

Acton, Sax - from ake or oak town
Addis, Lat - from Ascia, an adze
Adelman, Sax - a gentleman
Addle, Sax - to reward, to earn
Aidon - the wing of an army
Ailesford, Sax - the eagle's ford
Akers, Sax - acres of land
Alder, Sax - elder or first
Aldworth, Sax - old walk
Alley, Fr - allee, a lane or path
Ancaster, Sax - a castle
Arondel, Fr - a swallow
Askew, Teut - disdain or crooked
Ayling, Sax - sickly
Aye, Sax - for ever
Banbury, Sax - city of slaughter
Bandon - a company or retinue
Bane, Sax - a murderer or slayer of men
Barkly, Sax - land of birch trees
Baily - a magistrate apptd to keep peace
Barrow, Sax - a little hill or mount
Basnet, Lat - a helmet
Baxter - a baker
Bayard - a bay horse
Bawrel - a hawk
Beauchamp, Fr - a good & fair field
Beaufort, Fr - a commodious and fine port
Beauly or Bewley, Fr - a pleasant place
Beaumont, Fr - a pretty mount
Behen, or Behn - a kind of wild fruit
Beverly, Sax - Bede's abbey
Barton, Sax - a farm or barn for barley

Bevans, Welsh - from Ap Evans
Biggin, Fr - a religious order for women
Blout, Sax - dull, heavy, cowardly
Blundel, Fr - reddish haired or complexion
Bolt - a kind of herb
Bone - a boon or gift
Booth, Sax - a small cottage
Bourne, Sax - a river
Bowser - a purser
Bowyer - a maker of bows
Brackley, Sax - fern field
Brant, Sax - steep
Bartlett - derivation of Bartholomew
Brandling - a dew worm used for fishing
Brandreth - a fence or rail round a well
Branghwham - a dish of cheese, eggs, bread and butter
Brent - burnt
Brique - a dispute
Brigham - a horse collar
Bream - a fish
Bullen - hemp stalks peeled
Burt - a fish
Burrell - a fly
Buller - a bowler
Cade - a barrel or cask
Carr - a city
Cameline - a sort of Camlet
Campden - place of fighting
Caltrops, Sax - a weapon
Cob - a sea fowl
Cant - strong, robust
Cope - a hill
Capel - a horse
Casbery - a gooseberry

Chapman - a buyer or customer
Clough - a village between two hills
Colberts - tenants or villains made free
Castor - a purveyor of victuals
Collins or Collis - little hills or hillocks
Commyns - the common people
Coote - a waterfowl
Corbin - an offering
Corbet - a little crow
Cornell - a tree
Cottrell - a trammel to set a pot on the fire
Craven - a rock head
Cripps - from Crispin
Creswell - the broad edge of a shoe sole
Crotch - the forked part of a tree
Crouch - crooked or cross
Culver, Sax - a dove or pigeon
Canning - knowing cousins, kinsfolk
Dacre - a fowl
Dade - dazed or chilled
Darnef - the weed cockle
Dawkin - a slut
Denison - a foreigner
Dunne - a hill
Devereng - a town in France
Dighton - set off, drest to advantage
Donet - a grammarian
Eam - an uncle, compeer or friend
Eaton - a water town
Elden - fuel
Elves - morose, wicked
Fairfax - fair haired
Fane - a weathercock
Foulger - heath

Fuller - a cloth dresser
Fearon - frightened
Gabb - to prate
Gale - to bawl or laugh loudly
Galliard - merry
Gardeyne - a guardian
Garcia - a poor, servile lad
Gair - greedy
Gereves, Sax - guardians
Gledon - gone
Gladwin - an herb
Girthol - a sanctuary
Garth - a yard or little close
Godolphin - a white eagle
Guillam - a bird
Gurney - a Norman town
Graeme - anger, sorrow, mishap
Greaves - armour for the legs
Gresse, Lat - a stair or step
Grice - a young wild boar
Gurdon or Guerdon - reward, recompense
Harrow - Alas!
Hayne - hatred
Hopkins - from Robert
Hayward - keeper of the town cattle
Hanshaw - woodhaven
Huggins - from Hugh
Hockley - a dirty field
Hoolich - wholly
Hohn - a hill encompassed with fens or brooks
Holt - a small wood or grove
Hooper - a wild swan
Hoare - greyhaired
Hope - the side of a hill

Hogarth - high earth
Hodges, Hodgkins, Hoskins, Hodson - from Roger
Howlet - a little owl
Hoy - high - a lark
Howel - the sun
Hubert - clear colour
Hewlet - a crook
Huntley, Sax - hunt field
Hussey - a sordid garment
Ing - a meadow or common
Jennings, Jenkins - diminutives of John
Jordan - the river of judgement
Inke - to perch like a hawk
Kemp - a soldier
Keyns - a warder
Kennett - coarse welsh cloth
Kell - a kiln
Kersey - woollen cloth
Kuevels - linnets
Lea - a field
Lake - disgrace
Lammas - the 1st of Augst
Leke - lawful
Leman, Fr - sweetheart
Levett - a lesson on the trumpet
Levin - lightning
Limes - a bloodhound
Lisle - an island
Leche - a physician
Lever - better
Lorimer - a bit or harness maker
Loriot - a bird said to die when looked on by a jaundiced person &
     to effect the cure
Lovel - a little wolf

Lucas, Lat - of Luke
Lynne - to loiter
Madocks - a good one
Mahoune, Mahounes, Mahon - a turkish ship
Malpas - a bad way
Mainwaring - protector of men
Maie - a marsh or lake
Mather - a mower
Marmaduke - more mighty
Martinet - a kind of swallow
Mathurius - a religious order
Maynard - stout-hearted
Meyer - a marsh or bog
Merlin - a blackbird
Mitten - a measure of ten Bushels
Mollock - dirt, or dun
Moline - a mill
Moly - a kind of wild garlick
Mompesson - Mount Peterson
Mumford - a fortified mound
Montgomery - the gomers mount
Mortimer - dead sea
Mullins - from Moline
Moubray - a bread heap
Mynchen - a nun
Muns - the face
Murrey - moor coloured
Muscham - a moss field
Mordaunt - the tongue of a buckle
Montross - an under gunner or assistant engineer
Napier - a naperer
Nash - weak, tender
Neaving - barm or yeast
Neeld - a needler

Neville - Newtown
Noblay - nobility
Noel - natal
Norris - a nurse
Nuke - the back of the head
Oliphaunt - an elephant
Oughtred - noble counsel
Owen - from Eugene
Packer - a maker of merchants bales
Paine - endeavour
Paigles - cowslip flowers
Palmer - a pilgrim who carried a branch of palm
Palsgrave - a count or earl who has the oversight of a palace
Panton - a sort of horse shoe for narrow & low heels
Purdie - verily
Parker - a park keeper
Pen - a hill
Perdue - lost, forlorn
Peregal - equal
Price - a pit
Perkin & Peterkin - from Peter or Peterson
Petty - little, insignificant
Pomeyer - apple-tree
Pullen - poultry
Pinson - a shoe without heels
Pickett - sharp, nipping
Pollard - a chubfish
Plunkett - a sort of blue colour
Pomeroy - a fine flavoured apple
Pontifex - a high priest
Pope, Italian - pape! wonderful
Pooler - an instrument to stir up the Owfer of bark and water in tan-
   pits
Pomet, or Basuet - a skillet

Prevy - tame
Poynings - supporting
Powel - the son of Howel
Pritchard - the son of Richard
Powell - Howel's son
Prickett - a young male deer of the 1st year
Price - the son of Rice
Probert - the son of Robert
Proby - son of Roby or Robert
Progers - son of Roger
Pugh - the son of Hugh
Read - counsel, advice
Reeve - the bailiff of a manor
Rathe - early life
Ramsay - ram isle
Reeves - a tax gatherer
Rincy - hazy foggy weather
Rivers - of the banks
Romer - wider
Rouse - red-haired
Randle or Randall - from Ranulph
Rondle - tower at the foot of a bastion
Rou - ugly, froward
Row - a street
Ruding - inclining to a red colour
Rudge - the back of a sheep
Rundlet - a cask of 3 to 20 gallons
Reunet - a town in Normandy
Rymmer - a vagabond
Russell - dim. of Rousseau, somewhat red
Sanders - an Indian wood
Sasse - a sluice
Sartorius - a muscle of the leg
Scarsdale - rock valley

Selse - to stay
Sedwall, Sax - valerian
Seymour - St Maur
Seeley - hilly
Selby - a good habitation
Sentlow - St Loup
Sellenger - St Leger
Sentyn - scented
Seaton - a town by the sea
Shelfe - crooked
Sewell - what is set to keep deer out of any place
Shandy - wild
Shawe - a tuft of trees
Sheldrake - a water-fowl
Spink - a chaffinch
Sheath - the handle of a scythe
Simnel - a cake or bun of fine flour
Sherman - a shearer of stuffs
Sheriff - a shire reeve
Starkey - stiff
Stalker - a fowler or huntsman
Stanley - a stony field
Staple - a fair
Stannard - a tin mine
Sterling - easterling
Steedman - a horseman
Sterner - to lay down flat
Seward - a follower
Steven - sound, noise
Stowe - a place
Sturt - to straggle
Synclair - St Clair
Talbois - a carpenter
Tomkin - a bung or stopper

Talbot - a dog with a turned up tail
Teasil - a fuller's thistle
Takel - a feather
Teen - trouble, mischief
Tene - sorrow
Tyne - small, slender
Tinney - tawney
Terry - from Theodore
Tew - to tug or pull
Tegg - a doe in the 2d year
Traycey - traced
Thane - a nobleman, magistrate or freeman
Thorp - a village or country town
Tovey - half a bushel
Tozy - soft, like wool
Travers - a curtain
Trotters - curds
Troward - true of heart
Thurrill - a tool for coopers
Varley or Varlet - a yeoman's servant
Urling - an urchin, dwarf
Wakeman - a watchman
Ware - wary
Warrener - keeper of a warren
Wardle - watchfield
Warner - admonisher
Wattle - a sort of hurdle
Wagstaff - one who shakes or carries a staff
Wear - a dam to catch fish
Webster - a weaver or spinner
Were, Sax - a man
Wharre - crabapples
Wheatley - wheat field
Wheden or Weedon - a silly fellow

Whiniard - a scimitar
Whitaker - the north east part of a flat
Wiggins - sacred buildings
Wilcox - woodcock
Wyche - a farm
Windham - St Wimund's home
Winnets - vine branches
Withers - the shoulders of a horse
Woodruffe - a governor of a forest or town
Yates - gates
Welling - to flow or spring
Yourns - yours or belonging to you

Septr 14. 1828

Gaelic	Welsh
1. Aon	1. Un
2. Do	2. Dau
3. Tri	3. Tri
4. Cether	4. Peduar
5. Cuaec or coec	5. Pimp
6. Sia	6. Chuech
7. Seche	7. Sailh
8. Oche	6. Uilh
9. Naogh	9. Nau
10. Dec	10. Deg
11. Aoudec	11. Un ar deg
12. Dodec	12. Dau-deg
13. Tridec	13. Tri ar deg
14. Catherdec	14. Peduar ar deg
15. Cuaecdec	15. Pim-deg
16. Siadec	16. Un ar pim deg
17. Sechedec	17. Dau ar pim deg
18. Ochedec	18. Dau nau
19. Naoghdec	19. Peduar ar pim deg
20. Fighid	20. Ygen

— — — — — — — — — — — — — — —

Hungarian Superstition

He that is born in January should choose to wear a Garnet as that stone has a power over his destiny greater than he is aware of.

January. — Jacinth or Garnet. Denotes and ensures Constancy and fidelity in every engagement.

February. — Amethyst. Peace or Tranquility of mind.

March. — Bloodstone. Courage and Success in dangers & hazardous enterprises.

April. — Sapphire or Diamond. Repentance or Innocence.

May. — Emerald. Success in Love.

June. — Agate. Long life and health.

July. — Cornelian or Ruby. The forgetfulness or cure of evils effected by Friendship or Love.

August. — Sardonyx. Conjugal Fidelity.

Septr — Chrysolite. Preserves from or cures Folly.

Octr — Acquamarine or Opal. Misfortune or Hope.

Novr — Topaz. Fidelity in Friendship.

Decr — Turcoise or Malachite. The most brilliant success & happiness in every circumstance of life. The Turcoise has also the property of securing friendly regard; as the old saying, "He who possesses a Turcoise will always be sure of Friends"

1828

"The young Knights of the Bath on the day of their reception, clad themselves in rich silk mantles, to whose left shoulders were attached a double cordon or strings of white silk from which white tassels were pendant. This addition to the mantle was not regarded as a decoration, but a badge of gentle shame, which the knight was obliged to wear until some high emprise had been atchieved by him. The proud calls of his knighthood were remissible however by his Lady-love; for a fair and noble damsel could remove their stigma from his shoulders at her own sweet will; for there were no limits to woman's power in the <u>glorious</u> <u>days</u> of <u>Chivalry</u>."

"At the festival given in their honour the young Knights were permitted to sit down in their rich mantles in the King's presence but they were not allowed to taste any part of the entertainment for it was a feature in the simple manners of our ancestors that new made Knights and new made wives+ should be scrupulously modest and abstemious."

+ Thus Chaucer -

"A custom is unto these nobles all
A bride shall not eaten in the hall
Till days four, other - <u>three</u> <u>at</u> <u>the</u> <u>least</u>
Ypassed be, then let her go to feast."

Gavelkind, or the practice of dividing lands equally amongst all the male children of the deceased, was (according to Spelman) adopted by the Saxons, from Germany & is noticed by Tacitus in his description of that nation - <u>Gloss</u> <u>Archaiol</u>. folio. Lon: 1644

Harrison in his <u>description</u> <u>of</u> <u>England</u> prefixed to Hollinshed's Chronicle (Vol:1 p. 180) says "Gavelkind is all the male children equallie to inherit, & is continued to this daie in Kent, where it is onelie to my knowledge retained, & no where else in England." Lambarde in his descriptions of Kent thus notices it: - "The custom of Gavelkind is general and spreadeth itself throughout the whole shire, into all landes subject by ancient tenure unto the same, such places only excepted, where it is altered by Act of Parliament." ----

The following ext^t from Pinkerton's History of Scotland seems to have furnished Sir Walter Scott with the basis of his poem of "Halidon Hill" - "the Lady Elizabeth" there mentioned, he stated to be professedly a portrait of the Marchioness of Huntly ------

"Every singular tribute was paid to bravery during the famous battle of Homildon Hill - When the cloth yard arrows of the English yeomen were piercing the opposite line through and through, Sir John Swinton exhorted the Scotsmen not to stand like Deer to be shot at, but to indulge their ancient courage & meet their enemy hand to hand. His wish however was echoed by only one man, Adam Gordon, and between their families a mortal feud existed. Generously forgetting the hatred which each house bore to the other Gordon knelt before Swinton and solicited to be knighted by so brave a man. The accolade was given, and the two friends like companions in arms gallantly charged the English. If a kindred spirit had animated the whole of the Scottish line the fate of the day might have been reversed; but the two noble knights were only supported by about an hundred men-at-arms devoted to all their enterprises; and they all perished --."

— — — — — — — — — — — — — — —

The Normans brought with them into England civility & building, which though it was Gothic was yet magnificent. Upon any occasion of bustling in those days great Lords sounded their trumpets, and summoned those that held under them. Old Sir Walter Long of Draycot, kept a trumpeter who rode with thirty servants & retainers; hence the Sheriff's trumpets at this day.

No younger brothers then were to betake themselves to trade, but were churchmen or retainers of great men.

Vide - The Traditionary memoranda of Sir John Aubrey born in 1625 & distinguished as an antiquary & naturalist.

"London" - says May in his History of the Parliament "was at this time (1643) unfortified; nor could she, if the enemy, then master of the field, had come upon her, have opposed any walls, but such as those old Sparta used, the hearts of her courageous citizens. But now was begun the large intrenchment whch encompassed not only the city, but the suburbs on every side, containing about 12 miles circuit. That great work was by many hands completed in short time; it being the practice for thousands to go out every day to dig, all professions trades & occupations taking their turns not the inferior trades only but gentlemen of the best quality, Knights and Ladies! for the encouragement of others resorted to the work daily, not as spectators, but assistants, carrying themselves spades, mattocks & other suitable implements; so that it became a pleasant spectacle at London, to see them going out in such order and numbers, with drums beating before them, which put life into the drooping people, being taken for a happy omen that in so low a condition they yet seemed not to despair -"

Written on Leaving --- 1828

Adieu, my merry hearted friends! adieu with scarce a sigh
My absence will not cloud one brow nor dim one sparkling
    eye
We met in smiles - Why part in tears? In this brief world of
    ours
The natural sun should not be hid by artificial showers
It may be that in after times a thought may yet arise
Of all our merry summer freaks beneath the cloudless
    skies
And with a soft and painless sigh some rose-lipped girl
    may say
"I would that he were here tonight - that wild one far
    away -
"For if he were then not unmatched my laughing eyes would
    shine
"And not unpraised these foolish flowers among my hair
    would twine
"And not uncalled for be the song he lov'd so well to
    hear
"And not untold those whisper'd thanks - to woman's heart
    so dear"
But the pensive mood will soon be o'er, the mazy dance be
    wreathed
And not again for weeks, for months, will my poor name be
    breathed
'Tis strange - 'tis passing strange, how soon their
    places are filled up!
Though sparkle after sparkle dies on life's o'ermantling
    cup

We spent those golden days as if no parting hours would
    come
The voice of grief was never heard - of joy was never
    dumb
We parted - new friends will be found - -
Then they like me will pass away, & be like me forgot
And was there then not one, even <u>one</u> among the giddy
    throng
O'er whom a deeper spell was cast - a spell enduring
    long?
Does memory brood in no fond heart like wizard in his
    cell
A memory not of joy alone, but of its cause as well? -
Go, visit ye the festival, & cast your eyes around
Along the hall where music floats---
Is <u>every</u> ear intent to catch the minstrel's lively strain
Does <u>every</u> bounding step keep time to the pulse in ev'ry
    vein
Ay, by my faith! Above three days what woman ever pined
For out of sight with all the sex is to be out of mind?
Then adieu my merry hearted friends!
    Adieu with scarce a sigh
And long be yours the cloudless brow.
    The bright and laughing eye!

— — — — — — — —

When every voice of rapture woos
Thy charms, to share a happier part;
Ah Lady! wilt thou not refuse
The sighings of a broken heart?

And wilt thou, cold to every wile
Of promis'd bliss, that treasure cast
On love? which even amid thy smile
Will sometimes think upon the past?

Yet oh! regret not - 'twill not weep
New fondness; as, when storms are o'er,
The shipwrecked think upon the deep
To bless their sheltering home the more.

— — — — — — —

Saturday

In glowing terms I would this day indite
Its morn, its noon, its afternoon, its night.
The busiest day throughout the week - the latter day.
A day whereon odd matters are made even,

The dirtiest, cleanest too - of all the seven -
The scouring, pail, pan, plate & platter-day,
A day of general note and notability,
    A plague to gentlefolks
    And prime gentility.
E'en to the highest ranks - Nobility.
And yet a day (barring all jokes)
    Of great utility
Both to the rich as well as the mobility
A day of din, - of clack - a latter-day
For all, howe'er they mince the matter - say
    This day they dread.
(A day with hippish, feverish frenzy fed.)
Is that grand day of fuss and bustle -
    <u>Saturday!</u>

K. James VI of Scots is said to have had a particular predilection in
favor of this day for all important matters.

Sir Christopher Seaton (Ancestor of Alexr Seaton[x] who married Elizabeth daughter of Adam de Gordon 1398) bravely stood for the freedom of his country against the English usurpations and joined Robert the Bruce for the recovery of the kingdom and at the battle of Methven was one of those brave worthies that rescued King Robert out of the hands of the English and Scots rebels, as our historians & the English too, tell to their immortal glory. This piece of signal and eminent service endeared him much to the King, who gave him in marriage his sister Christian Bruce with whom he had issue.

He adhered to the King in all his troubles and at last had the ill-fortune to be taken by the English & carried to London, where with his brother John Seaton & his brother in law Nigel Bruce he and they were put to death by order of Edward 1st. King Robert after he had recovered & settled his kingdom in memory of the said Sir Christopher and of his lady, erected a Chapel near Dumfries that prayers might be said for their souls; the ruins of the chapel are yet known by the name of "Christal's Chapel". The charter of erection is to be seen in the Advocates Library Edinburgh.

[x] Isobel eldest sister of Alex Seaton married Sir John Stewart of Darnley, ancestor of Darnley and of Aubigny - the ancestor of the family of Lennox.

"The Floure of Souvenance"

The application of this name to the Myosotis Scorpiodis of botanists is of considerable antiquity; the story proves that the plant with its romantic association was known in England as early as the days of Edward III.

"Two lovers were loitering on the margin of a lake on a fine summer's evening when the maiden espied some of the flowers of the Myosotis growing on the water close to the bank of an island at some distance from the shore. She expressed a desire to possess them, when her knight in the true spirit of Chivalry, plunged into the water and swimming to the spot cropped the wished for plant but his strength was unable to fulfil the object of his atchievement, and feeling that he could not regain the shore, although very near it, he threw the flowers upon the bank, & casting a last look of affection upon his "Ladye love", he cried - "Forget-me-not!" - & was buried in the waters.

Anthony Todd Thomson - (the botanist who communicated this tale) says there are three varieties of this plant* "The one to which the tradition of this name is attached is perennial and grows in marshes & on the margin of lakes.

— — — — — — — —

* Myosotis Scorpiodis

Lines written on seeing a Caricature representing Eton and
Westminster weighed in a balance - the former kicking the beam
    What argues your device so rare
    Ye wits, of Eton jealous,
    But that your rivals soar in air
    And you are heavy fellows?
                  George Canning

Lines written on a paper tied round some pens that were sent by the
Duchess of Gordon to be mended by Dr. Beattie & returned to her
with them -
    Go, and be guided by the brightest eyes
    And to the softest hands thine aid impart
    To trace the fair ideas as they rise
    Warm from the purest, noblest, gentlest heart!

———————————

Lines written by Dr. Johnson to a lady
    Liber utesse velim suasisti pulchra Maria
    Ut maneam liber, pulchra Maria vale.
                  That translated -
    You urge me dear Maria to be free
    And that I may be so, farewell to thee.

———————

Translation

Rose, who displays't so peerless a mien
Of Flora's smiling offspring the Queen,
Thou, whom I chuse, this bosom to grace,
Shelterest midst thorns thy beautiful face

Spangled with dew-drops pearly and mild
Blushing adornest garden and wild
Sheddest e'en dying, Incense still free
Rose fair and blooming! Rose sweet perfuming!
Live thus, and die thus might I like thee.

J.H.C.

Our game of Backgammon seems to have had its origin thus - The words <u>Back</u> and <u>gammon</u> signify in the Welsh language an inferior kind of battle or contest.

The game of Backgammon was common in Wales so early as the tenth century.

Beddgelert - N. Wales

Llewelyn the Great, prince of Wales, is said to have had a hunting seat at this place. Among many others, he possessed one greyhound, a present from his father in law King John, so noted for excellence in hunting, that his fame was transmitted to posterity in four Welsh lines, which have been thus translated:

> The remains of famed Gelert, so faithful & good
> The bounds of the cantrel conceal
> Whenever the doe or the stag he pursued
> His master was sure of a meal.

During the absence of the family, tradition says, a wolf entered the house; and Llewelyn, who first returned, was met at the door by his favorite dog, which came out, covered with blood to salute his master on his arrival. The prince alarmed, ran into the nursery, & found his child's cradle overturned, & the ground flowing with blood. In this moment of terror, imagining that his dog had killed the child, he plunged his sword into his body and laid him dead upon the spot. But on turning up the cradle, he found his boy alive, and sleeping by the side of the dead Wolf. This circumstance had such an effect on the mind of the prince, that he erected a tomb over the faithful dog's grave; on the spot where afterwards the parish church was built called, from this incident, Bedd Gelert, or the Grave of Gelert. From this story was derived a very common Welsh proverb; "I repent as much as the man who slew his greyhound."

The following beautiful stanzas were written by the Hon. W.R.Spencer at Dolmelynllyn the seat of W.A.Madocks Esq. after a perusal of the story as related above

The spearmen heard the bugle sound
　　And cheerly smiled the morn
And many a brach & many a hound
　　Obey'd Llewelyn's horn.

And still he blew a louder blast
　　And gave a lustier cheer
"Come Gelert, come, wer't never last
　　Llewelyn's horn to hear

Oh! where does faithful Gelert roam,
　　The flower of all his race,
So true, so brave, a hound at home
　　A lion in the chace!"

'Twas only at Llewelyn's board
　　The faithful Gelert fed;
He watched, he served, he cheer'd his Lord
　　And sentinelled his bed.

In sooth he was a peerless hound
　　The gift of Royal John:
But now no Gelert could be found,
　　And all the chace rode on.

And now as o'er the locks and dells
　　The gallant chidings rise,
All Snowdon's craggy chaos yells
　　The many mingled cries!

That day Llewelyn little lov'd
    The chace of hart or hare,
And scant & small the booty prov'd
    For Gelert was not there.

Unpleas'd Llewelyn homeward hied,
    When, near the portal seat,
His truant Gelert he espied,
    Bounding his lord to greet.

But when he gained his castle door
    Aghast the chieftain stood,
The hound all o'er was smear'd with gore
    His lips, his fangs ran blood.

Llewelyn gaz'd with fierce surprise
    Unused such looks to meet,
His fav'rite check'd his joyful guise
    And crouched, and licked his feet.

Onward in haste Llewelyn past,
    And on went Gelert too,
And still where'er his eyes he cast
    Fresh blood gouts shock'd his view.

O'erturned his infant's bed he found,
    With blood stain'd covers rent
And all around the walls & ground
    With recent blood besprent.

He call'd his child no voice replied,
　　He searched with terror wild
Blood, blood he found on every side
　　But nowhere found his child.

"Hell hound! my child's by thee devour'd,"
　　The frantic father cried,
And to the hilt his vengeful sword
　　He plunged in Gelert's side.

His suppliant looks, as prone he fell
　　No pity could impart,
But still his Gelert's dying yell
　　Pass'd heavy o'er his heart.

Arous'd by Gelert's dying yell
　　Some slumb'rer waken'd nigh: -
What words the parent's joy could tell
　　To hear his infant's cry!

Conceal'd beneath a mangled heap
　　His hurried search had missed
All glowing from his rosy sleep
　　The cherub boy he kiss'd.

Nor scaith had he, nor harm, nor dread
　　But the same couch beneath
Lay a gaunt wolf all torn & dead
　　Tremendous still in death.

Ah! what was then Llewelyn's pain!
    For now the truth was clear,
His gallant hound the wolf had slain
    To save Llewelyn's heir.

Vain, vain was all Llewelyn's woe
    "Best of thy kind, adieu!
"The frantic flow which laid thee low
    "This heart shall ever rue."

And now a gallant tomb they raise
    With costly sculpture deck't
And marbles storied with his praise
    Poor Gelert's bones protect.

There never could the spearman pass
    Or forester, unmov'd:
There oft the tear-besprinkled grass
    Lewellyn's sorrow prov'd.

And there he hung his horn & spear
    And there as evening fell
In fancy's ear, he oft would hear
    Poor Gelert's dying yell.

And till great Snowdon's rocks grow old
    And cease the storm to brave
The consecrated spot shall hold
    The name of "Gelert's Grave".

— — — — — — —

To my Birdie

Here's only you an' me Birdie - here's only you & me
    An' there you sit, you humdrum fool,
    Sae mute and mopish as an owl,
                Sour companie!

Sing me a little sang, Birdie - lilt me a little lay!
    When folks are here, fu' fair are ye
    To stun 'em with your minstrelsie
                The lee lang day.

An' now we're only twa, Birdie - an' now we're only twa
    'Twere sure but kind an' cozie birdie,
    To charm me wi' your hurdigurdie
                Dull care awa!

Ye ken, when folks are pair'd Birdie - ye ken when
                      folks are pair'd
    Life's fair an' foul an' freakish weather
    An' light an' lumbering loads, thegither
                Maun a' be shared --

An' shared wi' loving hearts, Birdie - wi' loving hearts
                        & free
    Fu' fashions loads may weel be borne
    An' roughest roads to velvet turn,
                Trod cheerfully!

We've a' our cares and crosses, Birdie - we've a' our
                      cares & crosses!
    But then to sulk and sit sae glum-
    Hoot hoot, what gude o' that can come
                To mend one's losses?

Ye're clipped in wiry fence, Birdie - ye're clipt in wiry
                                    fence
  An' aiblins? - gin I mote gang,
  ? 'a wish - wad he, or lang
                            Wi' friends far hence.

But what's a wish? ye ken, Birdie, - but what's a wish?
                                    ye ken
  Nae cantrip haig like her's o' Fife
  Wha "darmit" wi' the auld wierd wife
                            Flood, fell and fen.

'Tis true ye're furnished fair, Birdie - tis true ye're
                                    furnished fair
  Wi' a braw pair o' bonnie wings
  Wad lift ye, where yon lavcock sings
                            High up i' th'air

But then that wire sae strang, Birdie - but then that
                                    wire sae strang
  And I myself sae seeming free
  Nae wings have I to waften me
                            Whar fain I'd gang!

An' say we'd baith our wills, Birdie - we'd each our
                                    wilfu' way!
  Whar lavcocks hover, falcons fly
An' say we'd baith our wills, Birdie -
  We'd each our wilfu' way!
  Whar lavcocks hover, falcons fly,
  An' snares an' pitfa's aften lie
                            Whar wishes stray.

An' aething weel I wot, Birdie
    An' aething weel I wot
    There's ane aboon the highest sphere
    Wha cares for a' his creatures here
                      Marks every lot --

Wha guards the crowned King, Birdie--
    Wha guards the crowned King,
    An' taketh heed for sic as me
    Sae little worth - an e'en for thee
                      Puir witless thing!

Sae now, lets baith cheer up, Birdie! -
    An' sin we're only twa
    Aff han' let's ilk ane do our best
    To ding that crabbit, canker'd guest,
                      Dull Care Awa!

To Scotland

My native land! my native land!
    How many tender ties,
Connected with thy distant strand
    Call forth my heavy sighs.

The rugged rock - the mountain stream-
    The hoary pine-tree's shade;
Where often, in the noon-tide beam
    A happy child I strayed!

I think of thee, when early light
    Is trembling on the hill;
I think of thee at dead midnight
    When all is dark and still!

I think of those whom I shall see
    On this fair earth no more
And wish in vain for wings to flee
    Back to thy much loved shore.

— — — — — — — —

O, Love! who bewailest
The frailty of all things here,
  Why choose you the frailest
For your cradle, your home and your bier."

Shelley

Georgiana Gordon
Jany 1st 1828

"Silence is the finest poetry at certain moments of Existence. The spirit hears it, and the Creator understands it -- that is enough."

What a world is the world of prayer!

What an invisible but all powerful tie is that of beings mutually known or unknown praying together or separately for each other! It has always seemed to me that prayer, that instinct so true of our powerless nature, was the only real force, or at least the greatest force of man! Man cannot conceive its effects - but what does he conceive? The want which drives man to breathe proves alone to him that air is necessary to his life! The instinct of prayer proves also to the soul the efficacy of prayer; let us pray then!

And thou, O GOD, who hast inspired this marvellous communication with thyself with beings and with worlds invisible, thou, O GOD, hear us favorably! let thy benignity surpass our desires!

As the power of the Spirit of God hovering over and troubling the face of the waters brought forth from chaos the beautiful form of Nature - So, the power of The Holy Spirit hovering over and agitating the polluted Soul will bring it forth, pure and acceptable from the chaos of Sin.

Revd James Buchanan

I hae naebody now - I hae naebody now
To meet me upon the green,
Wi' light locks waving o'er her brow,
An' joy in her deep blue e'en;
Wi' the soft kiss an' the happy smile
An' the dance o' the lightsome fay;
An' the wee bit tale o' news the while
That had happened when I was away.

I hae naebody now, I hae naebody now
To clasp to my bosom at even;
O'er her calm sleep to breathe the vow,
An' pray for a blessin' from Heav'n;
An' the wild embrace & the gleesome face,
In the morning that met mine eye!
Where are they now? Where are they now?
In the cauld cauld grave they lie.

O Dinna break my puir auld heart
Nor at thy loss repine;
For the unseen hand that threw the dart
Was sent from her Father and thine.
Yes, I maun mourn, an' I will mourn,
Even till my latest day;
For though my darling can never return
I shall follow her soon away.

1834

Just to her lips the cup of life she prest;
Found the taste bitter & refused the rest:
She felt averse to life's returning day,
And softly sighed her little soul away."
June 13: 1834

The Bedouins are fond of hearing stories after supper. This is one the Emir told us: it depicts the extreme attachment they have for their horses, and the self-love they manifest with regard to their own qualities.

One of his tribe, named Giabal, possessed a very celebrated mare. Hussad Pacha, then vizier of Damascus, made him on several occasions all sorts of offers to part with it, but in vain, for a Bedouin loves his horse as he does his wife. The pacha then employed threats, but with no better success. At length, another Bedouin named Ginfar, came to the pacha, & asked what he would give him if he brought him Giabel's mare? "I will fill thy barley sack with gold," replied Hassad who felt indignant at his want of success. This took place without transpiring (sic); and Giabel fastened his mare at night by the foot with an iron ring, the chain of which passed into his tent, being held by a picket fixed in the ground under the very felt which served him and his wife as a bed. At midnight Giafar creeps into the tent on all fours, & insinuating himself between Giabel and his wife, gently pushes first the one and then the other; the husband thought his wife was pushing; the wife thought the same of the husband; and each made room. Giafar then with a knife well sharpened, makes a slit in the felt, takes out the picket, unties the mare, mounts her, and grasping Giabel's lance, pricks him slightly with it, calling out, "It is I, Giafar who have taken thy noble mare; I give thee early notice!" and off he goes. Giabel instantly darts from the tent, calls his friend, mounts his brother's mare, & pursues Giafar for four hours. Giabel's brother's mare was of the same blood as his own, though not so good. Outstripping all the other horsemen, he was on the point of overtaking Giafar, when he cried out, "Pinch her right ear and give her the stirrup." Giafar did so, and flew like lighning. The pursuit was then useless the distance between them was too great. The other Bedouins reproached Giabel with being himself responsible for the loss of his mare.[x] "I would rather", says he, "lose her, than lower her reputation. Would you have me let it be said in the tribe of Would Ali, that any other mare has outrun mine?

I have at least the satisfaction of saying that no other could overtake her." He returned with this consolation & Giafar received the price of his address.

x Every Bedouin accustoms his horse to some sign when it is to put out all its speed. He employs it only on pressing occasions, & never confides the secret even to his own son.

"What a happy race are the Turks!

Their ashes always repose in the spot of their predilection, - beneath the shade of the tree or the shrub which they cherished in life, - on the bank of the current whose murmur has delighted them, - visited by the doves which their hands fed, and embalmed by the perfume of the flowers which they planted.

If they possess no portion of earth during life they possess it after death; they do not consign the remains of those they loved to charnel-houses, whence horror repels the worship and piety of remembrance."

Alphonse de la Martine

The Promulgation of Truth

We can never do more injury to Truth than by discovering too much of it on some occasions.

'Tis the same with understandings as with eyes: to such of a certain size and make, just so much light is necessary and no more. Whatever is beyond brings darkness and confusion. 'Tis real humanity and kindness to hide strong truths from tender eyes.

Shaftesbury

Some one else related that in the tribe of Hedgde there was a mare of equal reputation with that belonging to Giabal, and that a Bedouin of another tribe, named Daher, was almost mad with desire to possess her. Having in vain offered all his camels and his riches, he determined to stain his face with the juice of an herb, to clothe himself in rags, to tie up his neck and legs like a lame beggar & thus equipped to wait for Nabee, the owner of the mare, in a road by which he knew he must pass. When he drew near he said to him in a feeble voice: "I am a poor stranger: for three days I have been unable to stir from this to get food: help me and God will reward you." The Bedouin offered to take him on his horse, and carry him home; but the rogue replied: "I am not able to rise, I have not strength." The other, full of compassion, dismounted & brought the mare close , and placed him on her with great difficulty. As soon as he found himself in the saddle, Daher gave her a touch with the stirrup, and went off, saying - "It is I, Daher, who have got her, and am carrying her off."

The owner of the mare called out to him to listen: since that he could not be pursued he returned, and stopped at a short distance for Nabee was armed with his lance. He then said to him: "Thou hast my mare since it pleases God, I wish thee success: but I conjure thee tell no one how thou hast obtained her." "Why not?" said Daher. "Because some one really ill might remain without aid: you would be the cause why no one would perform an act of charity more, from the fear of being duped as I have been." Struck with these words, Daher reflected a moment, dismounted from the horse and gave her back to her master, and embraced him. Nabee took him home. They remained together three days and swore fraternity.

"Suffer little children to come unto me, and forbid them not, for of such is the kingdom of heaven."

This is the grandest tribute ever paid to the purity, to the happiness of childhood; a tribute we should ever remember when we mourn over the departure from this "vale of tears" of a lovely and interesting child, as a bud perishing in the morning: had that bud become a flower, without a covering from the inclement sky, the winds would have howled over its head, the dark clouds settled on its brow, and "in the evening, having lost some of its leaves and all its beauty, it would have sunk into the portion of weeds and outworn faces." But perishing in its morning, "twas but a piece of childhood thrown away." It had not to mourn over the gay hopes of the departed spring, and sigh for the reviving dews of the summer eve: no! it sunk as it rose with its soft and virgin modesty - pure & untainted.

"Tis gone & hopes are reconciled,
    Its little heart's at rest;
Death's angel read its name and smiled
    To find it with the blest."

"There are griefs so gentle in their very nature, that it would be worse than false heroism to refuse them a tear. Of this kind are the deaths of infants. Particular circumstances may render it more or less advisable to indulge in grief for the loss of a little child; but in general, parents should be more advised to repress their first tears on such an occasion, than to repress their smiles towards a child surviving, or to indulge in any other sympathy. It is an appeal to the same gentle tenderness, & such appeals are never made in vain.

The end of them is an acquittal from the harsher bounds of affliction, from the tying down of the spirit to one melancholy idea.

From the Italian of Petrarch

Bright days of sunny youth, irrevocable years!
 Period of manhood's prime,
O'er thee I shed tears unprofitable tears-
 Lapse of returnless time;
Oh I have cast away like so much worthless dross,
Hours of most precious ore-
Blest hours I could have coined for Heaven, your loss
For ever I'll deplore-
Contrite I kneel, O God inscrutable, to thee,
 High Heaven's immortal King!
Thou gavest me a Soul that to thy bosom free
 Might soar on Seraph wing:
My mind with gifts & grace thy bounty had endowed
 To cherish thee alone-
Those gifts I have abused this heart I have allowed
 It's Maker to disown.

But from his wanderings reclaimed with full with
        throbbing heart
 Thy truant has returned;
Oh! be the idol and the hour that led him to depart
 From thee for ever mourned
If I have dwelt remote, if I have loved the tents of
         guilt
 To thy fond arms restored,
Here let me die! on whom can my eternal hopes be built,
 Save upon thee, O Lord--

Humility the Mother of Charity

Frail creatures are we all! To be the best
    Is but the fewest faults to have;-
Look thou then to thyself & leave the rest
    To GOD, thy conscience and the grave.

Coleridge

"Les malheurs de la Société, les revers de la fortune, les chagrins de la disgrâce, les ennuis de l'exil, une famille reconnoissante et devouée peut tous adoucis!

Les blessures se ferment sous la beaume qu'elle y répand, les larmes coulent moins amères sous les mains consolatrice qui les assuient.

Oh! combien elle est plus nécessaire encore à l'infortuné condamner à subir la vie, quand il lui en reste à peine la sensation, et qu'il en a perdu le sentiment, quand le passé est pour lui sans souvenir, et l'avenir sans prévoyance; quand la raison absente luisse le coeur éteint, et qu'il ne reste de nous qu'un mort vivant auquel on ne peut rien prêter, pas même les larmes, et dont les tristes débris ne peuvent être soignés que pas la plus vive et courageuse tendresse!"

-- Legouvé - Ext^t d'une
oration funèbre

"Wherefore Children must hear truth, and not lies, be instructed with reason, not beaten with rods, advised with kindness, not threatened with words, presented with gifts, not crossed in toys, used with respect not slighted with neglect."

"Stripes create a spaniel's disposition, and timorous spirits, or hard and cruel natures - "

1834

O Frail as sweet! young bud, too rathe to bear
    The winter's unkind air;
O gift beyond all price, no sooner given
    Than straight required by Heaven;
Matchless jewel, vainly for a moment lent
    To deck my brow, or sent
Untainted from the earth, as Christ's to soar,
    And add one spirit more
To that dread band seraphic, that doth lie
    Beneath the Almighty's eye;-
Glorious the thought - yet ah! my babe, ah! still
    A mother's heart ye fill;
Though cold ye lie in earth - though gentle death
    Hath suck'd your balmy breath,
And the last kiss which your fair cheeks I gave
    Is buried in yon grave.
No tears - no tears - I wish thee not again;
    To die, for thee was gain
Ere Doubt, or Fear, or Woe, or act of Sin
    Had marr'd GOD's light within.

Oh, bonny is the laughing bairn
    While at its mother's knee
And little dreams its careless heart
    What weird it yet may dree.

Oh bonny is its rosy lip
    And its hair like rings o' gowd
And bonny is its bright clear e'en
    Like the tint o' the morning cloud.

But that rosie lip & that bright blue e'e
    Maun yet lie beneath the sod;-
Then may it take tenth o' the time to come
    An' gae spotless up to GOD.

                    Burns

Dirge

Calm on the bosom of thy GOD,
    Young spirit! rest thee now!
Ev'n while with us thy footstep trod
    His seal was on thy brow.

Dust, to its narrow house beneath!
    Soul, to its place on high!
They that have seen thy look in death,
    No more may fear to die.

Lone are the paths, and sad the bowers
    Whence thy meek smile is gone;
But oh! a brighter home than ours,
    In heaven, is now thine own.

               Felicia Hemans

"Friends are all very true when nothing is required of them beyond what is called friendship? but when you rely on them they bend, and ill brook supporting you."

— — — — — — — —

"What do I say? oh vanity of vanity, what is earthly friendship? Were a man to be restored to life a few years after his death I doubt whether those who shed the most tears when he expired, would then receive him gladly. So quickly do men form their connexions; so great is the inconsistency of man, and so short is our existence even in the memory of our friends."

Chateaubriand

"A just man is like a rock, that turns the wrath of all the raging waves into froth."

Presented with a Basket to the Editor
of a Country Newspaper
- by Thomas Miller - Basket Maker
33 St. George's Road, Southwark

Here osius by a murmuring river grew
That leaped & laughed in sunshine all the day
The winds thin lipped with their green leaves did play
And in their silvery palms their pearly dew
Hung like God-prest stars in night's deep blue
And birds sailed o'er them as the day grew grey
And white waves kissed their stems then rolled away
Singing a pleasant tune as on they flew

Despise them not - for 'twas a poet's hand
Gave them the simple form which now they wear
Better could he weave thoughts in accents bland
And by his power the heart in triumph hear
But he is a mere shell on ocean's strand
Which Triton's lip has not yet sounded clear.

Nov: 24, 1835

Shun delays, they breed remorse
Take thy time, while time is lent thee
Creeping snails have weakest force
Fly their fault lest thou repent thee.
Good is best when soonest thought
Lingering labours come to nought.

Hoist up sail while gale doth last
Tide & wind stay no man's pleasure
Seek not Time when time is past
Sober speed is wisdom's leisure.
After-wits are dearly bought
Let thy fore-wit guide thy thought.

Time wears all his locks before
Take thou hold upon his forehead
When he flies he turns no more
And behind his scalp is naked.

Works adjourned have many stays
Long demurs breed new delays.

Herrick

On hearing a Robin sing in Church during Divine Service - Nov. 1829

While grateful crowds their ready homage pay
And heavenly chauntings hail the sacred day
While the loud organ's note responsive swells
And the rapt soul in mute attention dwells
Say, little Robin, winter's sweetest bird
Shall thy small twitter waft its notes unheard?
Ah no! lone songster, humble though thy note
Though small the tribute of thy warbling throat
Yet in His eye, who marks the sparrows fall
Who ever present reigns the GOD of all;
To HIM, the feeblest song, the simplest prayer
To find an audit needs but to be sincere
Nor midst the skilful tones of human art
Wil he o'erlook the incense of the heart
But ever deign to lend a gracious ear
My hymns & thine sweet moralist to hear!

-o-o-o-o-

Come, Poverty to Pleasure's snares
To wild ambitions loftier cares
While calm content succeeds
Teach me stern goddess to deride
The miser's gold, the Monarch's pride
The Hero's boasted deeds!

Teach me while I no more pursue
The rainbow hope, which still in view
Still cheats the grasping fool
To shun the threshold of the great
No courtly sycophant, nor yet
Seditious faction's tool

Too long the dazzling glare
Where fortune with ambition sports
Drew my fond thoughts astray
Too long was pleasure's path my choice
While deaf to reason's sober voice
I heard her syren lay.

Ambition! Pleasure! fatal pair!
My buoyant spirits light as air
No gloomy damp opprest
Till soon by their delusive charms
I clasped them in my youthful arms
And press'd them to my heart.

'Twas then the poison they infus'd
Which through my inmost frame diffus'd
Mad passion's feverish rage -
But Poverty, though reason fail
With force resistless shall prevail
Its fury to assuage.

M.S.
Lord Glenbervie - 1769

"We're doomed to part, my Harp & I
And each must yield to destiny - "

Like the nightbreeze that comes o'er summer flowers
Thy strains have been to me in lonely hours
Heralds of Hope - soft soothers of Despair
Rapture to sense, - oblivion to care.
- But now we part, & I from other strings
Must draw forgetfulness of secret stings;
And thou, unmindful of the hands that strike
Will give to other hearts - to <u>all</u> alike
Those joys of sadness, that bewitching tone
Once sweet & sacred to my griefs alone.

- Oh! would that I, where'en I roam could gain
Like thee an audience to a soul-breathed strain
Give out the music of the mind within
Nor have each discord registered as sin.
Win from the world's great mart, a voice to heal
An ear to listen, and a heart to feel.
A voice that would not every sorrow blame
As though from wickedness or vice it came
An ear that would not gladly turn away
Or <u>seem</u> to listen, when in truth astray;
A heart though blessed itself, alive to feel
What <u>not</u> of <u>blest</u> another's could reveal.-

Yet I, like thee my Harp unmoved the while
By frown or keen critique or caustic smile
Like thee unmindful of the <u>who</u> or <u>where</u>,
The hands that touch thee, or the ears that hear,
Like thee, 'mid joy & revelry unblest -
Like thee, not useless, but like thee <u>at rest</u>.

But my poor Harp, if e'en we meet again
I shall but have to tell fresh tales of pain
I feel a prophet, while I say it must
Be so with me, though hope would whisper "trust".
Fears of a selfish world are now to me
What dews of dungeon vaults would be to thee,
Thy strings once like the fibres of my heart
Untuned, unequal to their former part
Thou wouldst be nothing. Gone-by lays would seem
The baseless fabrics of some lying dream
And thou wouldst feel (if feel thou couldst) the pain
Of memory on thee, as an iron chain.
Thy free-born spirit, by its ceaseless brave
Subdued, prostrated, changed into a slave!
- Oh thought of pain! the everlasting soul
Subjected to the fierce but weak controul
Of thread-like fetters!--

- Supreme Almighty mind - touch them with flame
- Let them no longer bind. --
As morning clouds by thy Empyrean ray
Let them be scattered; and a purer day
Shine on my mental vision, that my mind
Long with this rear-ward darkness all but blind
May now, and to the end, undazzled see
Truth, beauty, love & peace enthroned with thee.
May turn as it to mundane things before
Has turned with ardour - delve for brighter ore
And in the crucible of thought refine
All that it brings, till heart & soul are thine!

Miss S. Jones
1826

Chers enfans dansez, dansez
Votre âge échappe à l'orage
Par l'espoire gaîment bercés
Dansez, chantez, dansez.
A l'ombre de vastes charmilles
Fuyant l'école et les leçons
Petits garçons petites filles
Vous voulez danser aux chansons.
Envain ce pauvre monde
Craint de nouveaux malheurs
Envain le foudre gronde.
Couronnez vous de fleurs.
L'éclair silloune le nuage
Mais il n'a point frappé vos yeux
L'oiseau se tait dans le feuillage
Rien n'interrompt vos chants joyeux.
J'en crois votre allégresse
Oui, bientôt d'un ciel pur
Vos yeux brillans d'ivresse
Réfléchiront l'azur!

                                    1830

"The first in rank, & the first in talents can always afford to be freely liberal and kind -

They are the second-rates, who are obliged to look about them, and see lest something should be lost, in dignity and self-importance."

Extract of a letter from Rome
by Sir Thomas Lawrence P. R. A

Sur un beau site sur la rivière Clyde embelli par le propriétaire ami de l'auteur

— — — — — — —

Ces coteaux, autrefois, déserts et sans culture
Sont aujourdhui riants, tapissés de verdure,
Des chênes vigoreux, de superbes sapins,
S'élèvent, hardiment, du penchant des ravins,
Où croissoient le genêt, la rouce et la fougère,
S'erhalent, les parfums, de la fleur printanière;
Dès que le Clyde voit, de loin, ces beaux séjours
De ses rapides eaux, il détourne le cours,
Pour contempler l'effet de l'art sur la Nature;
Et les roulant alors, avec un lent murmure
Mollement se repose; attentif au doux chant
Des oiseaux réjouis de l'heureux changement
Il parcourt, à son gé, les beautés ravissantes,
De ces bords émaillés de mille fleurs naissantes,
Ornés, de peupliers, de platanes touffus
Dans un rang ombragé sur sa route étendus;
Mais, quand, en serpentant, vers Ganan, il s'avance,
Ou naguères regnoient la paix et l'abondance,
Indigné d'y trouver les arbrisseaux rompus
Les arbres, que ses eaux arrosoient, abattus
Et ces antiques tours, tristement solitaires
Des hiboux maintenant les dégoutans repaires
Il dédaigne, en ces lieux, de retarder ses pas,
Et s'enfuit écumant, avec bruit et fracas!

J.H.Christie - M.S.

Che faro senza Euridice?

I have lost my dear Eurydice
    She is gone! alas! for ever,
    Back to Pluto's drear domain
Never to return, ah! never!
    The grizly Stygian monarch to maintain
    Entire his dread primeval reign
    The forfeit fair will sure retain.
Dear Eurydice! darling Angel!
    Oh! do but answer
    Thy fond spouse, who calls in vain,
    One sad farewell to obtain:
    Dear Eurydice! dear Eurydice!

    Of my sole earthly joy bereft
    Not even of hope the solace left
    Doomed to drag life's galling chain
    Peace of mind I'll ne'er regain
For she is gone, my dear Eurydice,
    Back to Pluto's drear domain
    There for ever to remain
For evermore, ah! for evermore!

Translated by John Harvie Christie Esqre

"I merely perceived that I was considered intrusive, & finding in the company one who had treated me ill, I naturally supposed that he had prejudiced them against me. I hope I may be wrong; but I have seen so much of the world, young as I am, that I have become very suspicious."

("Then discard suspicion as fast as you can, it will)
(only make you unhappy, and not prevent you being)
(deceived. If you are suspicious you will have the)
(constant fear of deception hanging over you, which)
(poisons existence.")

"Still under the circumstances I can analyze the
(feeling - it is natural, but all that is natural is)
(not always creditable to human nature.")

"After these remarks I remained silent for some time; I was analyzing my own feelings, & I felt that I had acted in a very absurd manner."

Capt. Marryat. Japhet

The world is too much with us, late & soon,
Getting and spending, we lay waste our powers:
Little we see in Nature that is ours;
We have given our hearts away, a sordid boon!
This sea that bares her bosom to the moon;
The winds that will be howling at all hours,
And are up-gathered now like sleeping flowers;
For this, for everything, we are out of tune;
It moves us not. ------

Michael Angelo

To a Snow-drop

Lone Flower, hemmed in with snows & white as they,
But hardier far, once more I see thee bend
Thy forehead, as if fearful to offend,
Like an unbidden guest. Though day by day
Storms, sallying from the mountain-tops way lay
The rising sun, and on the plains descend;
Yet thou art welcome, welcome as a friend
Whose zeal outruns his promise! Blue-eyed May
Shall soon behold this border thickly set
With bright jonquils, their odours lavishing
On the soft west-wind & his frolic peers;
Nor will I then thy modest grace forget,
Chaste snow-drop, vent'rous harbinger of Spring
And pensive monitor of fleeting years!

Wordsworth

------- "Festivities are fit for what is happily concluded; at the commencement they but waste the force and zeal which should inspire us in the struggle and support us through a long continued labour. Of all festivities the Marriage Festival appears the most unsuitable; <u>Calmness</u>, <u>Humility</u> & <u>silent Hope</u> befit no ceremony more than this."--

Goethe

"What is it that keeps men in continual discontent &
agitation? It is, that they cannot make realities
correspond with their conceptions, that enjoyment steals
away from among their hands, that the wished-for comes
too late, and nothing reached and acquired produces on
the heart the effect which their longing for it at a
distance led them to anticipate."

"It is with talents as with virtue; one must love them for
their own sake, or entirely renounce them."

"Nothing is more touching than the first disclosure of a
love which has been nurtured in silence, of a faith grown
strong in secret, & which at last comes forth in the hour
of need, and reveals itself to him who formerly has
reckoned it of small account."-

Goethe

"A well-bred carriage is difficult to imitate; for in strictness it is negative; & it implies a long continued previous training. You are not required to exhibit in your manner anything that specially betokens dignity; for by this means you are likely to run into formality & haughtiness. You are rather to avoid whatever is undignified and vulgar. You are never to forget yourself are to keep a constant watch upon yourself and others; to forgive nothing that is faulty in your own conduct; in that of others neither forgive too little or too much."

"The well-bred man of rank, in spite of every separation, always seems united with the people around him; he is never to be stiff or uncomplying he is always to appear the first, & never to insist on so appearing. It is clear, then, that to seem well-bred a man must actually be so. It is also clear why women are generally more expert at taking up the air of breeding than the other sex; why Courtiers and soldiers catch it more easily than other men."

Goethe

"Corvisart". said the first Consul, "is it possible that a child should die of grief, in consequence of no longer seeing some one it loves, its nurse for example?

"I believe not," said C. "at the same time it is not impossible. I have in my portfolios a multitude of notices relative to the affections of children, & if you should read them General you would find not only that the germs of the passions exist in their young hearts, but that in some children these passions are developed in an alarming manner. Jealousy, for example will kill, as with poison, children of three years and even younger."

"You think then that this little Junot has died of grief from ceasing to see his Father?" asked the first Consul. "After what Madame has stated I cannot doubt it; and my conviction is confirmed by her having without being aware of it, described all the symptoms of that malady of which only beings endowed with the most exquisite sensibility are susceptible."

"This child is then happy in its early death; he would have been to be pitied throughout his existence, and would have met with a perpetual succession of disappointments." -

I do not love Thee, no! I do not love thee
And yet when Thou art absent I am sad
And envy e'en the darkening sky above me
Whose quiet stars obey Thee and are glad.

I do not love Thee, yet when Thou art nigh
Whate'er thou dost seems most well done to me
And often in my solitude I sigh
That those I do love are not more like Thee.

I do not love Thee, yet when Thou art gone
I seek thee as tho' Thou wert truly dear
For Thou my Saviour art, and Thou alone
Canst save me from the terrors which I fear.

I do not love Thee, yet thy searching eyes
Through all th'expanse of heaven's ethereal blue
Can see the thoughts as in my breast they rise
And judge of all the ways I ever knew.

I know I do not love Thee, and yet alas!
'Tis Thou alone canst cleanse my sinful heart
And teach the fleeting moments as they pass
To bring me nearer where thou art.

Septr 3. 1830

E:D.G.....

Like the low murmurs of the secret stream
Which through dark alders winds its shaded way
My suppliant voice is heard - Ah! do not deem
That on vain lays I throw my time away

In the recesses of the forest vale
On the wild mountain - Or the verdant sod
Where the fresh breezes of the morn prevail
I wander lonely - communing with GOD

When the faint sickness of a wounded heart
Creeps in cold shudderings through my sinking frame
I turn to Thee - that holy peace impart
Which soothes th'invokers of Thy awful name
Oh all pervading Spirit! - sacred beam!
Parent of life & light! Eternal power!
Grant me through obvious clouds one transient gleam
Of thy right essence in my dying hour.

Wm Bickford

I have trembled with emotion
Bending, at thy holy shrine
And, my heart's absorbed devotion
Lord, hath been entirely thine!

I have poured my soul before Thee
Spirit humbled on my knees
And have wakened to adore Thee
All my being's energies

I have laid my wearied head
On Thy sacred book of rest
Upon my quivering lips have read
The high promise of the blest,

Nature faints beneath the splendours
Of thine unveiled words of truth
While, to that sure pledge I tender
The deep homage of my youth:

Thro' the mists of earthly sorrow
I have raised mine eyes to Thee
And have marked a happier morrow
Bosomed in eternity.

There in ceaseless splendour beaming
Lie the scenes of blessedness
Floods of light, with rapture streaming
Glories, - nothing can express!

The heart knoweth its own bittercup, & a stranger doth
not intermeddle with his joy.

Prov XIV. 10

Why should we faint & fear to live alone,
Since all alone, so Heaven has willed we die[x]
Nor even the tenderest heart & next our own
Knows half the reasons why we smile & sigh!

Each in his hidden sphere of joy or woe
Our hermit spirits dwell and range apart
Our eyes see all around in gloom or glow -
Hues of their own fresh borrowed from the heart.

And well it is for us our GOD should feel
Alone our secret throbbings: so our prayers
May readier spring to Heaven, nor spend its zeal
On cloud-born idols of this lower air.

For if one heart in perfect sympathy
Beat with another, answering love for love
Weak mortals, all entranced on earth would lie
Nor listen for those purer strains above.

— — — — — — — —

[x] Je mourrai seul

Pascal

Or what if Heaven for once its searching light
Lent to some partial eye, disclosing all
The rude bad thoughts, that in our bosom's night
Wander at large, nor heed Love's gentle thrall?

Who would not shun the dreary uncouth place?
As if fond leaning where her infant slept,
A mother's arm a serpent should embrace.
So might we friendless live and die unwept.

Then keep the softening veil in mercy drawn
Thou who canst love us, tho' Thou reach us true,
As on the bosom of th'aerial lawn
Melts in dim haze each coarse ungentle hue.

So too may soothing Hope thy leave enjoy
Sweet visions of long severed hearts to frame,
Though absence may impair, or cares annoy
Some constant mind may draw us still the same.

We in dark dreams are tossing to and fro,
Pine with regret or sicken with despair
The while she bathes us in her own chaste glow
And with our memory wings her own fond prayer.

O bliss of child-like innocence and love,
Tried to old age! creative power to win,
And raise new worlds, where happy fancies rove
Forgetting quite this grosser world of sin.

Bright are their dreams because their thoughts are clear
Their memory cheering: but th'earth stained spright
Whose wakeful musings are of guilt and fear
Must hover nearer earth, and less in light.

Farewell for her, th'ideal scenes so fair-
Yet not farewell her hope, since Thou hast deign'd
Creator of all hearts! to own and share
The woe of what thou mad'st & we have stain'd.

Thou knows't our bittercup - our joys are thine,
No stranger thou to all our wandering wild:
Nor could we bear to think how every line
Of us, the darken'd likeness and defiled
Stands in full sunshine of thy piercing eye,
But that, Thou call'st us brethren: sweet repose
Is in that word - The Lord who dwells on high
Knows all, yet loves us better than he knows

— — — — — — —

"Thou hast known my soul in adversities

Ps. XXXI. 7

boy-

"The circles in which, in childhood, one may be compelled to move, may be esteemed low; the accidents all around him may be homely, the persons with whom we come in contact mean in appeal & sordid in nature: but his mind, if it remains to him pure as he received it from his Maker, is an unsullied gem of inestimable price, too seldom found and too little appreciated when found, among the great, or the fortuitously rich. Nothing that is abstractedly mental is low. The mind that well describes low scenery is not low, nor is the description itself necessarily so. Pride, & a contempt for our fellow creatures, evince a low tone of moral feeling, and is the innate vulgarity of the soul! it is this which but too often makes those who rustle in silks, & roll in carriages, lower than the lowest.

I have said this much, because the early, very early part of my life was passed among what are reproachfully termed "low people". If I describe them faithfully, they must still appear low to those who arrogate to themselves the epithet of "high". For myself I hold that there is nothing low under the sun, except meanness. Where there is utility there ought to be honour. The utility of the humble artisan has never been denied, though too often despised, and too rarely honoured; but I have found among the "vulgar" a horror of meanness, a self-devotion, an unshrinking patience under privation, and the moral courage, that constitute the hero of high life. I can also tell the admirers of the great, that the evil passions of the vulgar are as gigantic, their wickedness upon as grand a scale, and their notions of vice as refined, and as extensive, as those of any fashionable roue that is courted among the first circles, or even as those of the crowned despot. Then, as to the strength of vulgar intellect, - True, that intellect is rarely cultivated by the learning which consists of words. The view it takes of science is but a partial glance - that intellect is contracted but it is strong. It is a dwarf, with the muscles and sinews of a giant; & its grasp, whenever it can lay hold of anything within its circumscribed reach is tremendous. The general who has conquered armies & subjugated countries - the minister who has ruined them and the jurist who has justified both, never at the crisis of their labours have displayed a litle of the ingenuity & the resources of mind that many an artisan is forced to exert to provide daily bread; or many a shopkeeper to keep his connexion together, and himself out of the workhouse. Why should the exertions of intellect be termed low in the case of the mechanic, and vast, profound, glorious, in the case of the minister? It is the same precious gift of a benificent Power to all his creatures. As well may the sun be voted as excessively vulgar, because it, like intellect, assists all equally to perform their functions. I repeat that nothing that has mind is, of necessity, low, and nothing is vulgar but meanness."

"Allow me the poor consolation of contemplating what I might have been. There is piety in the thought. There is in it a silent homage to the goodness of the Creator, in acknowledging that he gave me purity & high capabilities of virtue: & there is hope also, for perhaps, at some future time, if not here, hereafter, that soul may again adore Him, in all the infant purity in which he bestowed it, ere I was, in a manner, compelled to sin. I am, after years of suffering, no more than a shell, but now corroded & shattered, that is cast upon the sands. At times I think that not all the former bright tints are defaced and that if the breath of kindness be breathed into it gently, it is still able to discourse, in return, some few notes of "most excellent music".

Recollections of Ralph Rattlin

The Poetry of the Psalms
by Felicia Hemans

This was the last effort of the amiable poetess & muse.

Nobly thy song, O Minstrel! rushed to meet
Th'Eternal on the pathway of the Hast,
With darkness round him, as a mantle cast,
And cherubim to waft his flying seat
Amidst the hills that smoked beneath his feet
With trumpet-voice thy spirit call'd aloud,
And bade the trembling rocks his name repeat,
And the bent cedars, and the bursting cloud:
But far more gloriously to earth made known
By that high strain than by the thunder's tone,
The flashing torrents, or the ocean's roll,
Jehovah spoke, thro' thee imbreathing fire,
Nature's vast realms for ever to inspire
With the deep worship of a living soul.

— — — — — — —

Alfonso II is a very interesting character among the Kings and Knights of Spain - Whatever share he might have had in his Brother Sancho's death such foul conduct did not sully his general dealings.

Justice was so admirably administered in Castille during his reign AD 1065–1070, that the people expressed their joy in the beautiful sentence - "that if a woman were to travel alone through his dominions , bearing gold and silver in her hand, no one would interrupt her path - whether in the desert or the peopled country - "

Thomas Moore's song of "Rich & rare were the gems she wore - " is professedly taken from an old Irish tradition to the same effect - a proof of the Spanish Ancestry of part of the Inhabitants of Erin - though I doubt of the fact of the Spanish saying being applicable to the state of Ireland - at least present times would seem to discredit it.

William Taylor residing at Old Moss near the old house of Gight parish of Fyvie, now in his 97th year related to Mr Manson the present minister of this place, that he remembers being on the hill near Rothie Brisbane with his Father herding when his Father espied the <u>redcoats</u> advancing and sent him then a gay <u>gangerel</u>[x] to tell his Mother to put her chickens & other poultry in a place of safety - The precaution was in vain for the Troops speedily "potted them a' " spite the guid wife's care - This happened on a Friday and on the Sabbath following when Taylor's Father took him to the Kirk of Fyvie they saw the Troops busily engaged "at the cartes[#] in "Gight's laft" - or family pew -

[x] gangerel - a trot about - [#] cartes - a game of cards

The above William Taylor is nearly related to the Nethermuir Gordons, and brother of the late Minister of Old Deer.

There are at present living in this parish which contains 3.200 inhabitants - Three individuals upwards of ninety years of Age - William Taylor ninety-seven in perfect possession of all his faculties and in good health - a woman of ninety-six, bed-ridden, and another a widow aged ninety-three in active good health - thirty-seven individuals who have attained eighty years and upwards and about two hundred persons above the age of seventy.

Fyvie Castle
October 3. 1836.

— —

Inscription on a triple gold ring found at Auchindoon Castle supposed to have belonged to Adam de Gordoun

Hart be kynd have me * in mind
As I have the * gentil hart is myne
It * sal be thyne and evir sal be *

o-o-o-o-o-o

Death is here & Death is there,
Death is busy everywhere,
All around, within, beneath,
Above is death - & we are death.

Death has set his mark & seal
On all we are and all we feel,
On all we know and all we fear,

   x x x x x x x x

First our pleasures die - and then
Our hopes, & then our fears - and when
These are dead, the debt is due,
Dust claimed dust - and we die too.

All things that we love and cherish
Like ourselves must fade & perish,
Such is our rude mortal lot,
Love itself would, did they not.

      Shelley

On a Faded Violet
Song

The odour from the flower is gone,
    Which like thy kisses breathed on me;
The colour from the flower is flown,
    Which glowed of thee, and only thee!

A shrivelled, lifeless, vacant form
    It lies on my abandoned breast,
And mocks the heart which yet is warm
    With cold and silent rest.

I weep -- my tears revive it not!
    I sigh -- it breathes no more on me;
Its mute and uncomplaining lot
    Is such as mine should be.

To-Morrow

Where art thou, beloved, To-morrow?
Whom young & old & strong and weak,
Rich and poor, through joy and sorrow,
Thy sweet smiles we ever seek,-
In thy place - ah! well a day!
We find the thing we fled - To-day.

Shelley.

A Lament

Oh, world! oh, life! oh, time!
On whose last steps I climb.
 Trembling at that where I had stood before;
When will return the glory of your prime?
 No more - Oh never more!

Out of the day and night
A joy has taken flight;
 Fresh spring, & summer, & winter hoar,
Move my faint heart with grief, but
 with delight No more-
  O, never more!
  --- o ---

Sonnet

Ye hasten to the dead! What seek ye there?
Ye restless thoughts & busy purposes
Of the idle brain, which the world's livery wear
Oh thou quick Heart which pantest to possess
All that anticipation feigneth fair!
Thou vainly curious mind which wouldest guess
Whence thou didst come, & whither thou may'st go,
And that which never yet was known would know
Oh whither hasten ye that thus ye press
With such swift feet life's green & pleasant path
Seeking alike from happiness and woe
A refuge in the cavern of grey death?
Oh heart, and mind, and thoughts!
                    What thing do you
Hope to inherit in the grave below?

- - - - With his child I played;
A lovelier toy sweet Nature never made;
A serious, subtle, wild, yet gentle being;
Graceful without design and unforeseeing;
With eyes -- speak not of <u>her</u> eyes! which seem
Twin mirrors of Italian Heaven, yet gleam
With such deep meaning as we never see
But in the human countenance
             With me
She was a special favourite, I had nursed
Her fine & feeble limbs when she came first
To this bleak world;   x   x   x   x
      x   x   x   x   x   x   x
      x   x   x   x   x   x   x

To a Child

I saw thee in thy opening bloom
    Of beauty and of glee
Untouched by sorrow's chilling gloom
    From care's dominion free
Who then could prophecy the doom
    Reserv'd by Heaven for thee?

Joy shook the ringlets round thy brow
    And lit thy hazel eye
Heightened thy cheek's transparent glow
    Thy lips carnationed dye
And swelled thy bosom's pride below
    Untaught as yet to sigh.

Joy was around thee and it seemed
    To all when thou wert nigh
As if, retired from life, they dreamed
    Of happier worlds on high
And thee a guardian seraph seemed
    The brightest in the sky.

No one could think of death and thee
    As things at all akin
In thee the holiest could not see
    One taint of primal sin
So peaceful was the purity
    That dwelt thy form within

No more on earth thy footsteps move
   Thy joyous voice no more
May stir our hearts with notes of love
   Till our full souls run o'er
To bless thee as we'd bless the dove
   The olive branch that bore.

Yet still when night's dark clouds descend
   And oft on lonely days
My minds eye on the past I bend
   Thy well loved form to raise
Thy lip's glad accents to attend
   And meet thy joyous gaze

                  Fabre d'Eglantier

L'Amour

Passer ses jours à désirer
Sans trop savoir ce qu'on désire;
Au même instant rire et pleurer

Sans raison de pleurer et sans raison de rire
Redoubter le matin et le soir souhaiter
    D'avoir toujours droit de se plaindre
    Craindre quand on peut se flatter
    Et se flatter quand on doit craindre
    Adorer, haïr son tourment
A la fois s'effrayer, s'irriter des entraines
Passer légèrement sur les affaires graves
    Pour traiter un rien gravement.
Se montrer tour à tour, dissimulé, sincère
Timide, audacieux, crédule, méfiant;
    Trembler, en tout sacrifiant,
    De ne point encore assez faire.
    Voir des rivaux en ceux que l'on doit estimer
    Etre le jour, la nuit, en guerre avec soi-même
    Voilà ce qu'on se plaint de sentir quand on aime
    Et de ne pas sentir quand on cesse d'aimer.

Dufresnoy

To ----------

One word is too often profaned
    For me to profane it
One feeling too falsely disdained
    For thee to disdain it.
One hope is too like despair
    For Prudence to smother
And Pity from thee more dear,
    Than that from another.

I can give not what men call love
    But wilt thou accept not
The worship the heart lifts above
    And the Heavens reject not,
The desire of the moth for the star
    Of the night for the morrow,
The devotion to something afar
    From the sphere of our sorrow?

— — — — — — —

To -- -- --

Mine eyes were dim with tears unshed;
    Yes, - I was firm - thus wert not thou;-
My baffled looks did fear yet dread
    To meet thy looks - I could not know
How anxiously they sought to shine
With soothing pity upon mine.

To sit & curb the soul's mute rage
    Which preys upon itself alone;
To curse the life which is the cage
    Of fettered grief that dares not groan
Hiding from many a careless eye
The scorned load of agony.

While thou alone, then not regarded
    The (--) thou alone should be,
To spend years thus, and be rewarded
    As thou sweet love, requited me
When none were near - Oh! I did wake
    From torture for that moment's sake

Upon my heart thy accents sweet
  Of peace and pity, fell like dew
On flowers half dead; - thy lips did meet
  Mine tremblingly; thy dark eyes threw
Thy soft persuasion on my brain,
Charming away its dream of pain.

We are not happy, sweet; our state
  Is strange & full of doubt and fear;
More need of words that ills abate;-
  Reserve or censure come not near
Our sacred friendship, lest there be
No solace left for thou and me.

Gentle & good and mild thou art,
  Nor can I live if thou appear
Aught but thyself, or turn thine heart
  Away from me, or stoop to wear
The mask of scorn, although it be
To hide the love thou feel for me.

Jeremiah   C. XXXV. v 15.

Hark, the voice of loud lament
    Sounds through Ramah's sadden'd plain!
There cherished grief, there pining discontent,
    And desolation reign.
    There amid her weeping train
See Rachel for her children mourn
    Disconsolate, forlorn!
    The Comforter she will not hear
And from his soothing strains she hopeless turns her ear
    Daughter of affliction peace,
    Let at last thy sorrows cease,
    Wipe thy sadly streaming eye,
    Look up, behold thy children nigh:
Lo! thy vows have all been heard,
See how vainly thou hast feared!
See from the destroyer's land
Comes the loved, lamented band
Free from all their conquered foes
Glorious shall they seek repose:
Sweet hope for thee remains,
Smile at all thy former pains:
Joy shall with thy children roam,
And all thy gladdened bowers shall bloom.

"Pierre de Terrail, or Bayard was born in 1476 at the Chateau of Bayard in Dauphiny. His family was of ancient & noble races, & boasted that their ancestors had fought at Cressy and Poictiers. In 1501 Charles VIII granted him a device having for its emblem a porcupine with the words "Vires agminis unus habet". - When he was page to the Duke of Savoy, he loved an attendant of the Duchess, but the passion was either not mutual or not graced with any character of romance, for some years after the damsel married the Seigneur de Fleurpas. Bayard met her at the house of the widow of the Duke of Savoy. During supper the lady of Fleurpas praised the chivalry of her early admirer, in such high terms that he blushed for very modesty and she added that as he was now residing in the family which had been the first to cherish him, it would be great blame in him if he did not prove himself as gallant a Knight as he had before. The answer of Bayard was that of a polite cavalier, for he requested her to tell him what he could do to please the good & honorable assembly - his Lady of Savoy - and her fair self. She advised him to hold a tournament. "Vraiment" dit le bon chevalier "puisque le voulex il sera fait. "Vous estes la dame en ce monde qui a premièrement réquis mon coeur à son service, par le moyen de votre bonne grace. Je suis assuré que je n'en aurai que la bouche et les mains, cas de vous requérir d'autre chose je perdrois ma peine: aussi sur mon âme j'aimerois mieux mourir que vous presser le déshonneur. He then prayed her to give him one of her sleeves for he said he should require it in the approaching tournament. The lady accordingly took it from her dress and he attached it to his. The martial pastime was held and after the supper it was enquired - to whom should the prizes (the sleeve the ruby) be given. The Knights accorded it to Bayard. But he declared the honor was not his, but if he had done anything well Madame de Fleurpas was the cause as she had given him her sleeve. He therefore prayed that she might be permitted to act according to her own judgement & prudence. The Seigneur de Fleurpas knew too well the noble caracter of Bayard to feel any jealousy at this compliment to his wife, but with the other

173

judges of the tournament he went to her & related the matter. She was delighted at Bayard's gallantry & declared as he had done her the honor to avow that her sleeve had made him gain the prize, she would preserve it all her life for the sake of his love. The ruby she gave to the Cavalier who had distinguished himself next to Bayard.

And thus lived "Le chevalier sans peur et sans reproche" till the retreat of the French from Italy in 1524 when he was fatally wounded by a stone from an Arquebuse. He fell from his horse crying "Jesus my Saviour, I die!" He kissed the cross handle of his sword & there being no chaplain present confessed himself to his esquire who then by the Knight's command placed himself against a tree with his face towards the enemy; "because" said Bayard, "as I have never yet turned my back to the foe, I will not begin to do so now." The Constable of Bourbon as he was pursuing the French found him in this state & assured him of his pity, but Bayard replied "It is not I who need pity, but you who are carrying arms against your King, your country & your oath!" After a while he was removed to a tent & shriven by a Priest, & soon afterwards died, as with true Christian piety he was imploring GOD & his Saviour to pardon his sins, and to shew him mercy rather than justice. He was buried at a Convent of Mimius, half a league from Grenoble, the principal town of his native country.

Translation of Mémoires de Bayard 1825.

vide Ancient Hymn to the Graces

"The doctrine of universal harmony seems rather to have been illustrated & established than invented by Pythagoras; it attributes all the perfection and imperfection all the virtue and vice, all the happiness and misery that are found among men, to the greater or lesser degree of harmony.

Thus, with respect to the fine arts - as music depends upon the harmony of sounds, so does sculpture on the harmony of forms, and Painting on the harmony of lines and colours. In the same manner, the greater or lesser degree of happiness enjoyed by any individual is in proportion to the harmony that reigns amongst his passions, and it is in consequence of the joining and dissonance of our feelings that we are unhappy.

Sudden shocks and violent emotions, by throwing the mind out of its balance or equipoise, either stun the frame of man or agitate it, and then all pleasing ideas, all gracious feelings are lost to us. Immoderate gaiety and deep grief are therefore unknown to the Graces: those deities sometimes smiling with a chastened joy, sometimes sighing with gentle compassion make man from time to time recollect that he has been entrusted to the alternate care of Pleasure & Sorrow as to two guides, who are to support him with a straight & even course through his allotted share of life. Pleasure gives him strength & courage to endure the chastening hand of Sorrow, by whom he is to be taught the path to virtue and glory"-

Ugo Foseolo

175

'Tis o'er - in that long sigh she past -
Th'enfrachised spirit soars at last!

And now I gaze with tearless eye
On what to view was agony
That parting heart is tranquil now
And Heavenly calm that ruffled brow,
And those pale lips that feebly strove
To force one parting smile of love,
Retain it yet - soft, placid, mild,
As when it grac'd my living child!

Oh! I have watched with fondest care,
    To see my opening flow'ret blow
And felt the joy which parents share
    The pride which fathers only know.

The spoiler came, yet paused as though
    So meek a victim checked his arm,
Half gave, and half witheld the blow
    As forced to strike yet loath to harm.

We saw the fair child's fading bloom,
The ceaseless canker-worm consume
    And gazed on hopelessly,
Till the mute suffering pictured there
Wrung from a father's lips a prayer
Oh GOD! - the prayer his child might die!

Ay, from his lip - the rebel heart
E'en then refused to bear its part.
But the sad conflict's past - tis o'er
That gentle bosom throbs no more!
The spirit's freed - through realms of light
Faith's eagle glance pursued her flight
To other worlds, to happier skies;
Hope dries the tear which sorrow weepeth
No mortal sound the voice which cries
"The damsel is not dead but sleepeth!"

— — — — — — — —

Alexander Gordon 1st Earl of Huntlie for his 3d wife married Elizth Crichton dr of the Chancellor of Scotland & entailed his estate on the heirs male procreate betwixt them two and of <u>their male successors</u>. She had to him 3 sons,- George, 2d Earl of Huntlie - Alexander of Midmar ancestor to the Abergeldies - Adam, dean of Caithness and Rector of Pillie he was a man of good learning & governed the Diocese of Caithness 24 years he had 3 sons and 1 daughter - William the eldest son was Chancellor of Dunkeld - George the second son of Beldorney was ancestor of the family of Wardhouse John the 3d son was called of Drummoy - Elizabeth his daughter m. Lord Findlater - The Earl died at Strathbogie July 15, 1479 & was buried in the Cathedral Church of St. Peter Elgin, in the aisle dedicated to our lady - or St. Mary - his lady died also at Strathbogie in 1497 & was also interred at Elgin.

Buchanan the poet tho' a declared enemy to the family of Gordon, being conscious of his great merit long after his death wrote on him the following epitaph

Clausus Alexander iacet hac Gordonius urna,
Qui priscum ornavit lumine stemma novo
Forma decens firmae vires, unoque tenore
Continuo nullis sors labefacta malis.
Dives opum, luxuque carens, dona hospita cunctis
Pectus amans pacis, fortis ad arma manus.
Omnia permensus felicis commoda vitae
Hic animam coelo reddidet ossa solo.

-------- O --------

The monument still stands & the inscription legible; during the troubles the silver head which was placed on the stone effigy was carried off & the figure still remains headless - 1828.

"A person under the power of love, or fear, or anger, great pain, or deep sorrow has so little government of his soul that he cannot keep it attentive to the proper subject of his meditation.

The passions call away the thoughts with incessant importunity toward the object that excited them, and if we indulge the frequent rise and roving of passions we shall thereby procure an unsteady and inattentive habit of mind.

Yet this one exception must be admitted, viz if we can be so happy as to engage any passion of the soul on the side of the particular study which we are pursuing, it may have great influence to fix the attention more strongly to it.

It is therefore very useful to fix & engage the mind in the pursuit of any study by a consideration of the divine pleasures of truth and knowledge by a sense of our duty to God - by a delight in the exercise of our intellectual faculties - by the hope of future service to our fellow creatures and glorious advantage to ourselves both in this world and that which is to come.

These thoughts though they may move our affection yet they do it with a proper influence, these will rather assist & promote our attention than disturb or divert it from the subject of our present and proper meditations.

A soul inspired with the warmest love of truth and the warmest aspirations after sincere felicity and celestial beatitude, will keep all its powers attentive to the incessant pursuit of them; passion is thus refined and consecrated to its divinest purposes."

------------- "Excess in the studies of learning or the business of life, or its amusements or dissipations, may overwhelm the memory by overstraining & weakening the fibres of the brain, overwasting the spirits and injuring the true consistence of that tender substance and confounding the images that were laid up there."

Watts

"It is a singular fact, that the imbecile are, in general extremely attentive to their own interest, & perhaps most commonly cautious in their proceedings. Ruinous extravagance, absurd schemes, & quixotic ideas of liberality and magnificence are more allied to insanity; The former may become the dupes of others, but it is the latter who are most likely to involve and ruin themselves."

J.H.

"If you would know what sort of companions you should select for the cultivation & advantage of your mind -- choose such as, by the brightness of their parts and their diligence in study, or by their superior advancement in learning or peculiar excellence in any art or science or accomplishments, divine or human, may be capable of administering to your improvement, and be sure to maintain and keep a due regard to their moral character always, lest while your mind is in quest of intellectual gain you fall into contagion and vice."

"O ye, whom struggling on life's craggy road
With obstacles and dangers, secret foes
Supplant, false friends betray, disastrous rage
Of elements of war, of civil broil
Bring down to Poverty's cold floor, while grief
Preys on the heart and dims the sinking eye
Faint not! - There is who rules the storm, whose hand
Feeds the young ravens, nor permits blind chance
To close one sparrow's flagging wing in death.
Trust in the Rock of Ages. Now even now
He speaks, and all is calm. Or if, to prove
Your inmost soul, the hurricane still spread
Its licensed ravages, He whispers hope,
Earnest of comfort, and through blackest night
Bids keen eyed Faith on Heaven's pure sunshine gaze
And learn the glories of her future home."

Gisborne

Inscription in the Hall at Aston
The residence of James Watt

"If service be thy means to thrive
Thou must therein remaine
Both silent, faithful, just, and true
Content to take some paine.

If love of virtue may allure
Or hope of worldly gaine
If fear of God may thee procure
To serve do not disdaine."

Aston Hall was built by Sir Thomas Holte about 200 years ago - being commissioned in the reign of James & finished in that of Charles. In front it has a terrace 700 feet long & 50 broad fronting which is a pannelled gallery 130 feet in length.

An attack was made on this ancient mansion by Oliver Cromwell, the traces of which still remain. One of the shot carried away part of the railing of the staircase, & lodged in the wall opposite -

J.B. June 9 -1834

The Welsh language even as now spoken has more sounds agreeing with the Hebrew than all the other languages together.

Hebrew	Welsh	English
Bagad	Bagad	A great many
Barek	Bara	Meat or victuals
Cir	Caer	A fortified place
Cis	ˣCist	A chest
Denak	Dyna	This or That
Gad	Cad	An army
Gadah	Gadaw	To pass by
Gavel	Gafael	Tenure or bounded lands
Geven	Cefyn	A ridge or back
Hanes	Hanes	To signify or account
Jissal	Isel or Iselu	To throw down
Mah?	Mae?	What? Where? How?
Maguur	Magwyr	A habitation or dwelling
Malas	Melys	Sweet or to sweeten
Mar	Maer	A Lord
Meab	Mab	A Son
Mohal	Moel	A hill
Nadu	Nadu	They moan
Nafe	Nef	Joyful
Path	Peth	A part or portion
Reith	#Rhith	Appearance
Sac	Sack	A Sack
Sethar	Sathrir	To throw under the feet

ˣ The word Kist is commonly used for Chest both in Scotland and parts of Yorkshire

Wraith or Raith is used in Scotch to designate an apparition or spirit.

Welsh	English
Ni, nyni	We, us two-
Nyein, nyn.	Of us two-
Oio	To think, to bear in mind

--------o--------

The Pearl Muscle is found in the river Ithan or Ython -
Aberdeenshire - I have seen several large and beautiful specimens of
the pearls -- #

Mya Margaritifera

Gen: Cha: Shell Bivalve gaping at one end, Hinge with a broad thick
tooth, not let into the opposite valve. Specific Characters. Shape Oval
bending in on one side.- Shell thick opake & heavy. Tooth of the hinge
smooth & conical - Length 5 or 6 inches breadth 3/4

By a strange coincidence the river Ithon in Wales also possesses the
pearl muscle in abundance.

A short time since died, near Turriff, Banffsh. having attained the remarkable age of 132 years John Gordon. All the travellers who chanced to call at the neighbouring Inn of Turriff were uniformly directed by the landlady Mrs. Wallace to the cottage of the patriarch, where they would see (she used to say) the oldest man in Banffshire "ay, or in the world". Among the visitors one day about the close of harvest was a young Englishman who coming up to the door of the cottage, accosted a venerable looking man, employed in knitting hose, with "so my old friend, can you see to knit at your advanced period of life? one hundred and thirty-two is truly a rare age." "De'ils i' the man " it will be my grandfather ye're seeking - I'm only seventy three - ye'll find him round the corner o' the house." On turning round the corner the stranger encountered a debilitated old man whose whitened looks bore testimony to his having long passed the meridian of life, and whom the stranger at once concluded to be John Gordon himself. "You seem wonderfully fresh, my good sir, for so old a man; I doubt not but you have experienced many vicissitudes in the course of your very long life." "What's your wull, sir?" inquired the person addressed whose sense of hearing was somewhat impaired. The observation was repeated. "Oh, you'll be wanting my father, I reckon - he's i' the yard there." The stranger now entered the garden where he at last found the venerable old man busily employed in digging potatoes, & humming the ballad of the Battle of Haclan.

"I have had some difficulty in finding you friend as I successively encountered your grandson and son, both of whom I mistook for you; indeed they seem as old as yourself. Your labour is rather hard for one of your advanced age." "It is (replied John) but I'm thankfu' that I'm able for't, as the laddies, puir things, are no very stout now."

December 21. 1837

The Holly Tree

O Reader! hast thou ever stood to see
    The Holly Tree?
The eye that contemplates it well perceives
    Its glossy leaves
Ordered by an intelligence so wise
As might confound the Atheists' sophistries.

Below a circling fence, its leaves are seen
    Wrinkled and keen;
No grazing cattle thro' their prickly round
    Can reach to wound;
But as they grow where nothing is to fear
Smooth and unarm'd the pointless leaves appear.

I love to view these things with curious eyes
    And Moralize!
And in the wisdom of the Holly Tree
    Can emblems see
Wherewith perchance to make a pleasant rhyme
Such as may profit in the after-time.
So, tho' abroad I might appear
    Harsh and austere,
To those who on my leisure would intrude
    Reserved and rude
Gentle at home amid my friends I'd be
Like the high leaves upon the Holly Tree.

And should my youth, as youth is apt I know
    Some harshness shew,
All vain asperities I day by day
    Would wear away
Till the smooth temper of my age should be
Like the high leaves upon the Holly Tree.

And as when all the summer trees are seen
    So bright and green,
The Holly leaves their fadeless hues display
    Less bright than they.
But when the face of wintry woods we see
What then so cheerful as the Holly Tree.

So serious should my youth appear among
    The thoughtless throng
So would I seem amid the young & gay
    More grave than they,
That in my age as cheerful I might be
As the green winter of the Holly Tree.

             Jany 1. 1828

Honesty is like a strong perfume: one little grain of it suffices to enrich a great mass, that had neither scent nor value before.

How little honesty is there in the world! and, yet, what numbers of men, that by some or other, are termed honest.

Bishop Jebb

The Sabbath

"It is no rash assertion, that from that holy institution, the Sabbath, have accrued to man more knowledge of his GOD, more instructions in righteousness, more guidance of his affections, & more consolation of his spirit, than from all other means which have been devised in the world to make him wise and virtuous. We cannot fully estimate the effects of the Sabbath, unless we were once deprived of it. Imagination cannot picture the depravity which would gradually ensue if time were thrown into one promiscuous field without those heaven directed beacons of rest to direct the passing pilgrims. Man, would then plod through a wilderness of being, & one of the avenues which now admits the light that will iluminate his path, would be perpetually closed.

Bishop Delion

Oh! I could gaze for ever on this scene
And pour my spirit forth to Nature's God!
For here his breath is felt - his presence seen;
There could I wish to sleep beneath the sod!
And here, my soul made holy and serene
By nature's influence, would make her abode,
And mix, where every evil thought must cease,
'Mong hallowed spirits in a world of peace.

Octr 1826 - Glenfiddich

x x x x x
Then patient bear the sufferings you have,
And by these sufferings purify the mind,
Let Wisdom be by past misconduct learn'd
Or pious die, with penitence resigned.

Collins

Notes

72   Tom Paine (1737–1809) is perhaps best known for his pamphlet "Common Sense" and for his "Rights of Man" (published in 1791 as a reply to Burke's "Reflections on the French Revolution"). These works are what O'Connor is referring to in the second stanza. Paine lived at various times in England and America, and in France, where he was returned to the National Convention by the electors of Pas-de-Calais.

When Charles Fox (1749–1806) entered the House of Commons as a supporter of Lord North (1733–1792) "his success was immediate, and was the more readily assured since he took the side of the majority". However he later became a violent opponent of North, particularly in respect to American policy. Eventually the breach was healed, superficially at least, when they became colleagues in a Coalition Government. (Ref. 10 of Introduction).

88   The Battle of Homildon Hill took place in 1402, so the Lady Elizabeth mentioned by Scott could not have been the Marchioness of Huntly, the 1st Marquis having been created in 1599. The name Elizabeth appears to have been popular at the time. The mother of the Adam Gordon slain at Homildon Hill was Elizabeth Keith, daughter of Sir William Keith, 7th Great Marshall of Scotland. Adam's sister Elizabeth married Sir Alexander de Seton, who became head of the Gordon clan. Their son was created 1st Earl of Huntly. The surname of the third Lady Elizabeth is a matter of conjecture. In "Halidon Hill" Scott has Gordon whispering the name to Swinton, who responds "I know it well, that ancient northern house." Scott writes that there was an obvious reason for transferring the scene of action from Homildon to Halidon Hill; — "for who would again venture to introduce upon the scene the celebrated Hotspur, who commanded the English at the former battle?" He also pointed to a number of similarities: the English victories, the decisive role of the long-bow in each case, a Gordon being left on the field of battle and the same circumstances of mismanagement on the part of the vanquished, on each occasion the Scots having been commanded by "an ill-fated representative of the House of Douglas" (J.L.Robertson, Ed. "Scott — Poetical Works", Oxford University Press, first published 1904).

90   These events appear to refer to the period of the Civil War when London was being defended by the parliamentary forces under the Earl of Essex. The Royalist forces had their headquarters at Oxford, and were in control at Reading until April 1643, when the town fell to the parliamentarians. About a year later the Royalists, commanded by the young and impetuous Prince Rupert, were defeated at Marston Moor, and after another year Charles himself was defeated at Naseby, and fled the field.

91   This would have been written at the time Georgiana was leaving Gordon Castle to live in Edinburgh, after the death of Alexander, the 4th Duke of Gordon.

95   Bruce's sister, referred to here as Christian, is usually known as Christina.

97   George Canning (1770–1827) was educated at Eton and Oxford. He was British Prime Minister in the last year of his life, after long and distinguished service to his country. He was a follower of Pitt the Younger, and the two laboured in 1799 to effect the union with Ireland, on the basis of equal political rights for Catholics, but they were unable to overcome the King's opposition, and both resigned. Of Pitt's successor, Addington, Canning said "Pitt is to Addington as London to Paddington" (Ref. 10 of Introduction). Canning's name is perpetuated in British colonies established shortly after his death, for example, in Western Australia, in the main tributary of the Swan River.
    The Duchess addressed by Dr Beattie is of course Jane Maxwell, first wife of the 4th Duke of Gordon.

100 Brach — female of hound

101 Gouts — spots, drops

109 This is where the notebook starts again (from the other end).

113 This is clearly an expression of Georgiana's grief at the death of Elizabeth in 1834 (see Introduction). For some time afterwards Georgiana was obsessed with the death of children, as shown by the entries on pages 114, 120, 121, 126 and 176.

118 Historians are divided on the character of the Earl of Shaftesbury, Macaulay apparently accepting Dryden's satirical description:

> For close designs and crooked counsels fit
> Sagacious, bold and turbulent of wit;
> Restless, unfixed in principles and place,
> In power displeased, impatient of disgrace,

but Christie ("Life of Shaftesbury") and Ranke ("History of England") adopting a much more charitable interpretation of his activities.(Ref.10 of Introduction)

124 "Beaume" appears to be an older spelling of "baume" (balm). Georgiana has written "oration" (last line). The usual word is "oraison".

125 "Stripes" is obscure, but the word is unmistakable.

127 Weird — fate

128 Felicia Dorothea Hemans, née Browne (1794–1835) married Captain Hemans in 1812; they separated after six years, and "she devoted herself to a life of literary toil to provide means to educate the five sons left dependent on her exertions"(Bellew, ref.11 Introduction).

Perhaps she is best remembered for the poem beginning "The stately homes of England" and for "Casabianca":

> The boy stood on the burning deck
> Whence all but he had fled;
> The flame that lit the battle's wreck
> Shone round him o'er the dead.

137 "Enfans", "brillans" are older forms of "enfants", "brillants".

139 The words in lines 5, 18 and 19 are clearly "croissoient", "regnoient" and "arrosoient" respectively, presumably older forms of the ending "-aient". "Naquères" is now spelt without an "s".

141 This is from "Japhet in Search of a Father", the story of a child of unknown parents who eventually achieved prosperity. Captain Marryat was in the Royal Navy and most of his stories are about the sea (Prentice Hall Guide to English Literature, Ed. M. Wynne-Davies, 1990.)

142 "Michael Angelo" is of course the title of the sonnet, by Wordsworth. Georgiana has stopped in mid-line, after "It moves us not." Evidently she could not bring herself to follow Wordsworth into the next line with

> "...Good God! I'd rather be
> A Pagan suckled in a creed outworn, —"

148 The significance of this poem escapes us. "E:D.G" could be Elizabeth (Brodie), Duchess of Gordon, but who doesn't love whom or Whom is not at all clear. The poem, in a secularised form, is in The Oxford Book of English Verse 1250-1900 (Ed. A. Quiller-Couch), Clarendon Press (1916), the author being Hon. Mrs. Caroline Elizabeth Sarah Norton. The versions differ considerably, the printed one being

I do not love thee! — no! I do not love thee!
    And yet when thou art absent I am sad;
And envy even the bright blue sky above thee,
    Whose quiet stars may see thee and be glad.

I do not love thee! — yet I know not why,
    Whate'er thou dost seems still well done, to me
And often in my solitude I sigh
    That those I do love are not more like thee!

I do not love thee! — yet, when thou art gone,
    I hate the sound (though those who speak be dear)
Which breaks the lingering echo of the tone
    Thy voice of music leaves upon my ear.

I do not love thee! — yet thy speaking eyes,
    With their deep, bright, and most expressive blue,
Between me and the midnight heaven arise,
    Oftener than any eyes I ever knew.

I do not love thee! yet, alas!
    Others will scarcely trust my candid heart;
And oft I catch them smiling as they pass,
    Because they see me gazing where thou art.

151 Pascal actually wrote "On mourra seul" (Pensées, III, 211), quoted in "Concise Dictionary of Quotations", Collins, 1986.

156 It is interesting that Georgiana has labelled this poem "the last effort of the amiable poetess and muse". It is not to be found in "Hemans' Poetical Works" (Ward Lock and Co., London, undated but published well after Hemans' death). The poet visited Scotland in 1829, and was warmly received by Sir Walter Scott, with whom she spent a few days at Abbotsford. It is possible that she met Georgiana about this time.

161 In "Shelley's Poems and Essays and Letters from Abroad", edited by Mary Wollstonecraft Shelley and published in London in 1839, the first stanza of this well-known poem is given as follows:

> The colour from the flower is gone,
>   Which like thy sweet eyes smiled on me,
> The odour from the flower is flown,
>   Which breathed of thee and only thee!

Also, the word "shrivelled" in the second stanza has been replaced by "withered". This is a later version than that quoted by Georgiana (which was written in 1820) and more closely approaches perfection. Some of the changes are mentioned by T. Hutchinson in "The Complete Poetical Works of Percy Bysshe Shelley", Oxford University Press (first published 1905, reprinted many times).

163 Shelley, written in 1821. In Mary Shelley's book and in Hutchinson's (see Note for page 161 above) it appears under the same title, but in Palgrave's Golden Treasury it is under the Greek title "Threnos".

164 Shelley, written in 1820.

168 Georgiana, probably following Dufresnoy, has written "redoubter" (line 5). Modern French is "redouter".

169 Shelley appears to have written seven poems simply entitled "To....", of which this is perhaps the best known (See Mary Shelley, quoted in Note for page 161 above).

170 Also Shelley. See Note for page 169. The underlining, mainly on page 171, is by Georgiana.

177 Canker-worm (line 2): the same term is used by Shelley in the preface to "Adonais".

178 Georgiana has underlined the words "their male successors" in the fourth line. Is this an early manifestation of feminism?

The translation of the Latin epitaph has been kindly provided by Mr. Con Coroneos:

> In this urn lie the remains of Alexander Gordon who adorned with a new brightness his ancient heritage. He was graceful in form and robust in strength, and no crimes sullied his career. Rich in resources but free from luxury, he was hospitable to all. He had a peace-loving heart, but his hand was ready with weapons. Having lived through all that makes up a happy life, he has rendered his soul to heaven and his bones to the earth.

George Buchanan (1506-82), the writer of the epitaph, is remembered as a poet, classicist and educationalist, who mixed high scholarly endeavour with political intrigue (Prentice Hall Guide to English Literature). He was tutor to Mary Queen of Scots (whom he later helped prosecute for high treason), James VI and Montaigne. Most of his work, including love poems, was written in Latin.

186 Georgiana appears to have omitted some words after "de'il's i'", but we have not attempted to amend the passage.

190 Glenfiddich, famous for its whisky, is also a spot much admired for its beautiful scenery. Alexander, Georgiana's grandfather, also refers to it in his poetry.

Ancestors of Georgiana Huntly Gordon

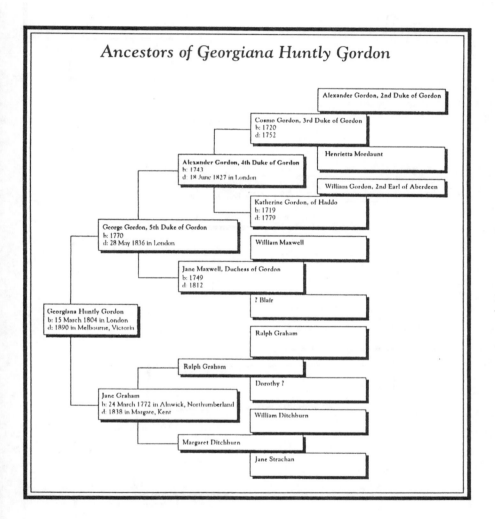

Ancestors of Andrew Murison McCrae

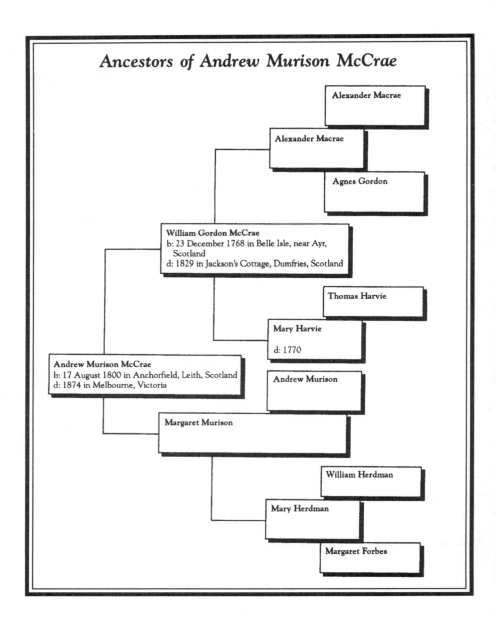

Alexander Macrae

Alexander Macrae

Agnes Gordon

William Gordon McCrae
b: 23 December 1768 in Belle Isle, near Ayr,
    Scotland
d: 1829 in Jackson's Cottage, Dumfries, Scotland

Thomas Harvie

Mary Harvie

d: 1770

Andrew Murison McCrae
b: 17 August 1800 in Anchorfield, Leith, Scotland
d: 1874 in Melbourne, Victoria

Andrew Murison

Margaret Murison

William Herdman

Mary Herdman

Margaret Forbes

Family of Alexander, 4th Duke of Gordon, 1743–1827

m. Jane Maxwell
Duchess of Gordon
1749–1812

Children
Charlotte
Duchess of Richmond
1768–1842

George,
5th Duke of Gordon
1770–1836

Madelina,
Lady Sinclair,
Mrs. C.F.Palmer
1772–1849

Susan,
Duchess of Manchester
1774–1828

Louisa,
Marchioness Cornwalis
1776–1808

Georgina,
Duchess of Bedford
1781–1853

Alexander Gordon
1785–1808

m. Jean Christie
Duchess of Gordon
1770–1824

Children
Catherine Anderson
1791–1847

Adam Gordon
1797–1834

Jean Macintosh
1801–?

Susan Gowdie Smith
1801–?

Charlotte Gordon
1810–1810

Others
(1) Bathia Largue

(2) Isobel Williamson

(3) ?

(4) Janet Reid
1798–1865

Children
(1) George Gordon
1766–1835

(2) Alexander Gordon
1794–1863

(3) Anne Gordon

(4) Jessie Robertson
1798–1865

201

Family of George, 8th Marquis of Huntly, later 5th Duke of Gordon, 1770–1836

m. Elizabeth Brodie	Ann Thomson	Jane Graham
1794–1864	1780–1862	1772–1838
No issue	**Children**	**Daughter**
	Admiral Charles Gordon	Georgiana McCrae
	1798–1876	1804–1890
	Susan Sordet	
	1805–1880	

The McCrae Family

Alexander Gordon McCrae   m.   Mary Harvie
("The Nabob")   d. 1770
1745–1796

William Gordon McCrae   m.   Margaret Murison
("The Liberator")   1770–1840
1768–1829   (sister of Sir A. Morison)

Children

Mary	m.	Francis Cobham
1797–?		
Captain Alexander McCrae	m.	Susannah Danway
1799–1871		
Andrew Murison McCrae	m.	Georgiana Gordon
1800–1874		1804–1890
John McCrae		
1804–1823		
Dr. Farquhar McCrae	m.	Agnes Morison
1906–1850		
Agnes	m.	William Bruce
1808–?		
Thomas Ann	m.	George Ward Cole
1810–1898		
Margaret	m.	Dr. David Thomas
1812–?		

Children of Andrew and Georgiana McCrae

Elizabeth Margaret McCrae 1831–1834

George Gordon McCrae 1833–1927   m.   Augusta Brown
    (Parents of the poet Hugh McCrae)

William Gordon McCrae 1835–1926

Alexander Gordon McCrae 1836–1923

Farquhar Peregrine McCrae 1838–1915   m.   Emily Brown

Georgiana Lucia 1841–1908   m.   Robert Hyndman

Margaret Martha 1844–1914   m. Nicholas Maine

Octavia Frances Gordon 1847–1941   m.   George Moore

Agnes Thomasina McCrae 1851–1854

Index